NASTY
BOSSES

NASTY BOSSES

WITHDRAWN

Jay Carter, Psy.D.

McGraw·Hill

New York   Chicago   San Francisco   Lisbon   London   Madrid   Mexico City
Milan   New Delhi   San Juan   Seoul   Singapore   Sydney   Toronto

The *McGraw·Hill* Companies

Library of Congress Cataloging-in-Publication Data

Carter, Jay.
    Nasty bosses / Jay Carter.
       p.   cm.
    ISBN 0-07-143247-7 (pbk. : alk. paper)
    1. Supervisors.   2. Managing your boss.   3. Personnel management.
  4. Interpersonal relations.   5. Supervision of employees.   I. Title.

    HF5549.12. C376   2004
    650.1′3—dc22   2004002057

1 2 3 4 5 6 7 8 9 0   AGM/AGM   3 2 1 0 9 8 7 6 5 4

ISBN 0-07-143247-7

Interior design by Nick Panos

McGraw-Hill books are available at special quantity discounts to use as premiums and sales promotions, or for use in corporate training programs. For more information, please write to the Director of Special Sales, Professional Publishing, McGraw-Hill, Two Penn Plaza, New York, NY 10121-2298. Or contact your local bookstore.

This publication is designed to provide accurate and authoritative information in regard to the subject matter covered. It is sold with the understanding that neither the author nor the publisher is engaged in rendering legal . . . or other professional service. If legal advice or other expert assistance is required, the services of a competent professional person should be sought.
       —From a Declaration of Principles jointly adopted by
a Committee of the American Bar Association and a Committee of Publishers

This book is printed on acid-free paper.

To good people managers,
including Nick and Daryl

Contents

Acknowledgments

Many thanks to the following people for their help with this book: My agent, Sherrill Chidiac, who helped and helped some more. My wife, Sheila, who once again put up with me through another book. My editor, Michele Pezzuti, who edited this book on her own time and did a great job. David Kramer, president and CEO of Domain, Inc., Julia Anderson Bauer, Nicole Chong, Bob Warner, Andy Herrmann, Mark Curry, Alex Cameron, J. R. Carter, Sue and Elizabeth in England, Brian Mehle, Dr. George Goodrich, Dr. Loretta Martin-Halpine, Ken Martin-Halpine, James Wo, Dr. David O'Connell, and the many people who gave me candid and confidential interviews who prefer not to be mentioned.

From the Author

This book consists of things I have been developing for decades as well as recent information from the horse's mouth (executives, managers, and people in high places).

I have laid out the principles in this book in lectures and workshops, and I've seen people absorb and utilize the perspectives and explanations described. What I've set out to do in this writing is give you useful "big picture" tools for surviving and thriving in your corporate environment, no matter what your employee level or management level, and to gain confidence in yourself, your self-worth, and your goals. In this book you will learn some of the following:

1. The executive function model (very enlightening)
2. The mammal mentality (temperament, etc.)
3. How to identify and effectively deal with the types of bosses

The principles people find most enlightening and comforting are these:

1. The squeeze (You are not alone. We are all made to experience this in one way or another.)
2. Thinking out of the box with regard to organizations (Getting creative in corporate America means getting creative in creating coping mechanisms that work for you.)

You will find that the combination of real-life common sense and sound psychology meld together into a practical psychology for you to use. It gives you a real edge in today's business world. I am interested in your feedback, and there is information about how to contact me at the end of the book.

I have a unique background. I retired from IBM management after twenty-six years and then became a psychologist. I am a witness to the changes in organizational behavior that have occurred over forty years. I am a business consultant and have done personality testing and studies and have participated in reorganizations. I have friends and relatives in high places who give me the straight scoop and who give me the means of meeting others in strategic positions. So it is what I know *and* who I know that enable me to write this book. While I was a manager at IBM, I had excellent morale and was very successful in meeting the goals of my organization(s). Only one of my superiors understood my subtle low-key approach. The rest of my superiors thought I was just lucky. I was lucky for so many years . . . consistently. What a run! You will find the keys to some of my "luck" in this book (understanding people, thinking out of the box, donning a workable perspective, and taking responsibility).

I would change only one thing, if I had to do it over. I would have shared my approach with my management and spent more time with my management so that my success would have been attributed to something more than luck. Communication is still the number one secret to success. I got by on the number two secret to success—taking total responsibility—and the number three secret to success—seeing the big picture and what really matters through the forest of small detail.

Introduction

The boss serves as the executive function for the group. He or she is the one who is supposed to see the big picture of the operation—the one who has vision and purpose. Psychologically speaking, the boss is the prefrontal lobe (PFL) of the group. The prefrontal lobe is that part of the human brain that is aware of the situation surrounding us and not just what is in front of us at the moment.

For example, right now you are reading this page, right? You are using your cognitive ability to be aware of this page. Ah, and you are also *aware* that you are *aware* of this page! Feel that? *That* is what separates us from the other mammals. We are self-aware and situationally aware. Children don't have this ability. It is one of the last potentials to develop in the brain. A child could be standing in front of a doorway with fifty people trying to get through, but the child may remain oblivious until someone says, "Hey! Get out of the way!" Research shows that the brain continues to develop into the late thirties. Coincidentally (or not so coincidentally), that's about the age that people start to think about the bigger picture. That's when they start thinking about retirement or what they want to accomplish in their lives.

The executive function (or "situational awareness") actually starts working (primitively) around the age of adolescence. Developmental theorists would say that this is when the adolescent develops the ability to think abstractly. When these functions start working in adolescence, the adolescent's parents suddenly seem to have a lower intelligence. Their IQs drop about forty points each (in the perception of the adolescent), and the parents don't get "smarter" until the adolescent is out of the teenage years. This newfound ability to perceive starts the adolescent questioning the parents' beliefs, discipline, and other things. The child has become self-aware and, in turn, other-aware.

Some children possess a situational awareness (executive functions) earlier in life. Dr. Alice Miller calls these children "gifted." These are children who seem to have an objective awareness at a very early age—a wisdom beyond their age and an ability to see a bigger picture. For most of us, the post office drops off this capability around adolescence. However, some people never open the package. In fact, research shows that 38 percent of the population are concrete thinkers, which means that they don't use the prefrontal lobe, where abstract thought originates. Personally, I think that the phrase "abstract thought" is a misnomer. It is more of an "awareness" than a "thought" process. The executive functions include "abstract thought," but the executive functions are all really "awarenesses" rather than thinking. For example, right now you are using your "thinker" to read this sentence, but your awareness is also operating, in that you know where you are in your environment. You are aware of what is going on around you, and you are aware of your situation (sitting in your home, riding the train, at the library, etc.).

The terms "boss" and "executive function" should be synonymous with a good prefrontal lobe function. The boss is supposed to be mindful of the bigger picture. The boss is supposed to have vision. The boss is supposed to see beyond the moment. The boss is the one who is supposed to think in terms of "relationships" rather than single interactions. He or she doesn't fire a good employee for one mistake. She or he doesn't take advantage of a customer who is likely to do future business. The boss is mindful of "reputation" in dealing with customers and employees. The *way* the boss deals with the bigger picture of things shows how much he or she has developed the executive abilities. A boss who is unable to have vision as to how a policy is going to affect customers, employees, or peers is a boss without insight and a boss who is headed for failure.

Personal ethics also plays a big role in a manager's ability to manage people. A boss who is not respected has greatly diminished power. We have seen this in presidents. It doesn't matter what kind of great things you have done; to many people, once you have sex with an intern without admitting it, or if you erase tapes, you can't be trusted. Once you see your boss treat someone unfairly, you feel that you may be next, and you have less trust and respect for the boss. This translates into less power for the boss because you are not so willing to go above and beyond the normal duties for someone who is going to then make you feel like a fool by treating you unfairly. These are human reactions to authority, and they will never change no matter what the company policy is. It all boils down to relationships. People who are screwing over other people usually don't have good relationships with those people, and some would prefer to go unseen by the people they are screwing over. Even Hitler couldn't bear to see the terrible things that he was doing to others. He would draw the window shades for fear that it would "weaken his resolve" (Payne, 1973). Some people see conscience as weakness. That kind of mentality ensures that they are on their way to their own personal hell. Don't go there with them. Each temperament is going to deal with a self-serving boss differently. Some are going to be confrontational. Some are going to avoid. The passive-aggressives are going to be happy if the boss trips and his nose connects with the floor.

There is a difference between ineffective bosses and nasty bosses, although there is a correlation with a nasty boss being a less effective boss. This doesn't mean that a good boss is a "nice" boss. (We are going to identify the qualities of a stereotypical good boss in Chapter 1.) A "nice" boss may give away the store, causing the operation to fail and people to lose their jobs. That isn't nice, really. But, there is never any good reason to be nasty and disrespect people—ever. There is never any good reason to be abusive to people—ever. I have never seen these qualities reap positive benefits in the long run. Can the boss be angry? Sure! Can the boss fire people? Sure. Does the boss have to do it disrespectfully and abusively? Absolutely not.

There was a man (we'll call him Joe) who had been working for a company for fifteen years. His boss thought he was a slacker. Joe did about two-thirds of the work that the other employees did, and sometimes the boss couldn't find him at his work location. The boss was a relatively new manager and was under a lot of pressure to get his department's productivity increased. The boss brought Joe into his office and interrogated him about his whereabouts in a sarcastic and demeaning manner. The boss leaned on him heavily and made snide remarks in front of Joe's peers. He brought the employee into his office weekly to question him about his low productivity and to invalidate him. Finally, the boss decided Joe needed to be fired. The company policy was to give an employee severance pay upon termination. This manager didn't want to comply and didn't think Joe should get any retirement. He told Joe that he didn't deserve anything because he had already "retired on the job" and was a "parasite" to the company.

Joe was a quiet man. During one of the weekly interrogations he had with his manager, Joe asked, "Don't you live out there on that lake outside of town?"

"Why?" asked the manager.

"Oh, just wondering," said the employee.

Here's where I come in. I was a peer manager at this company, and Joe's manager knew I had a background in psychology, so he came to me anxiously and asked, "Do you think this guy might come to my house and start shooting the place up?"

I told him I didn't think so, but everyone had limits. I told him I didn't approve of the way he was interacting with the employee. He told me he didn't want to give the guy something he didn't deserve (severance and retirement) and that Joe was a parasite who brought down the whole department. He couldn't just sit back and let this guy do whatever he wanted.

"No," I said, "I think you need to fire the guy, but do it respectfully."

"I have no respect for him," was his answer.

Then I asked, "Why do you respect people? Do you respect people because of who *they* are, or do you respect people because of who *you* are?"

He gave me a quick look, but he realized what I was saying. Then he had a moment without his ego present and said, "What would you do?"

I reminded him that this man had fifteen years with the company. This manager didn't know what he had accomplished during those fifteen years. He had gotten decent appraisals. I would do all the things the manager was doing (documenting him, telling him it was my intent to fire him, etc.), but I wouldn't disrespect him or abuse him. Who knows what is going on in this man's life? I would give him his severance pay. I would be empathetic that he couldn't hold up his productivity. I would ask if I could help him in any way. I would try to be respectful to this man . . . who was soon going to be without a job.

The manager took my advice. He continued to call Joe in weekly, but now the sessions were friendly, even with some joking and kidding. The manager acknowledged the employee for his past good appraisals. In the end, Joe still did not keep his productivity up, and so he was fired in a mutually agreeable way. There was no "violence in the workplace" that year for us.

Being nasty always causes more problems in the long run than it seems to accomplish in the short run. In this book I hope to demonstrate this.

Nasty Tactics

The tactics of a nasty boss are interesting.

1. **Yelling.** Yelling at an employee causes a stimulus response for many people, reminding them (unconsciously) of when they were a child and had to propitiate to an angry parent. It can be very effective for a nasty boss in the short run.
2. **The trilogy.** Then there is the "trilogy." You have seen it before: the ego, arrogance, and sense of entitlement that seems to come with a nasty boss. The boss's ego gets all fluffed up as when a cat

makes its fur stand on end and puffs up the chest. The arrogance makes for an appearance of righteousness or indignation or judgmental disgust. The entitlement is embellished to make you look like you owe the boss something and you haven't paid up.

3. **Threats and fear.** Fear is instilled through strategic threats, which can be verbal and nonverbal. Verbal threats usually indicate some potential punishment for your action or lack of action. They are within the power of the boss and sometimes have catastrophic implications for your career or employment (e.g., "If you don't meet that deadline, you'll never work in this town again"). They can be obvious (e.g., "If I don't have that on my desk in one hour, you will no longer *be* at your desk!!") or more subtle (e.g., "You know, I am trying so hard to show enough productivity so we don't get our workload transferred to India. I know you have a lot of unpaid hours already in, but this needs to be on my desk within the hour. I really would like to keep you employed, if I can."). Nonverbal threats are things like raised voice, standing over you, slamming things on your desk, stomping out of your work area, or making gross physical gestures.

4. **Snide remarks.** Snide remarks come as innuendos (e.g., "I guess you are too busy making personal calls to work on the project!") or state something in

a way that implies a "you dummy" after the statement (e.g., "Can't you see what has to be done here [you dummy]!?").

5. **Shame and embarrassment.** Adding shame or embarrassment to a statement (e.g., "Tsk. Tsk. Don't tell me you *still* don't have that done. Oh my!") has more of a negative effect when it is done with a raised voice in front of others.

6. **Mind-boggling.** Bosses may send mixed messages, "forget" promises made, and take actions that defy logic. (I have created the following scenario and dialogue to clarify what I mean by this.)

There was an executive manager who took over a branch office and immediately brought down the evaluation of all managers there to the lowest level, claiming that they couldn't possibly be appraised at a higher level if the branch was operating at such a low level. One of the managers asked, "So if we become an outstanding branch office, then we all get rated outstanding?" The executive thought for a minute, then said, "Sure." Well, that branch office ended up becoming the most outstanding branch office in the country in just over a year. The managers there all worked sixty hours a week and more to make it happen. The executive manager was then promoted out of the branch but came back to evaluate the managers and—surprisingly— gave them all the lowest evaluation. The instructions from *his* boss were to not give away the store, and he was a good soldier. And besides that, he attributed the success to *his* presence in the branch. Here is how one of the appraisals went:

Exec: It looks like you made twice the errors over the past year as you did in the previous year.

Manager: Yes, but I also did twice the work and the productivity-to-error ratio is still low.

Exec: Yes, but how is that going to look? I gave you a better appraisal for *twice* as many errors?

Manager: Yes, but because of the downsizing, I have twice as much responsibility and twice as many people. Look, I have busted my butt and had to put in sixty- and seventy-hour weeks to keep up.

Exec: I can't help it if you can't manage your time more efficiently.

Manager: Well, there was more work! Doesn't the *amount* of work have anything to do with it?

Exec: Well, I am not here to argue with you. Then there was that insubordination incident that I am going to do you a favor and not even mention.

Manager: What insubordination?

Exec: In my absence, I asked you to get the system shut down because I had a customer who needed a system change.

Manager: I tried to do that. There was no way they were going to shut down the entire system across the country for one customer of ours. Once I realized what it was, we would have looked stupid to request that and it would have affected their long-term attitude toward us. I saved you the embarrassment.

Exec: Well, you didn't do what I asked, but like I said, I am not going to report your insubordination.

Manager: Well how about the time I did what you said and forced a senior engineer to go out to a job with no sleep.

Exec: That's right. You shouldn't have done that even though I asked you to. You should've shown better judgment.

The manager had been highly respected for fourteen years and had made the correct decisions. And his negative evaluation wasn't personal. The exec gave such feedback to all the managers with the same mind-boggling techniques. He was very adept at making successful people feel like low-life, undeserving, inefficient failures. He was so brilliant that even someone with a decent self-esteem could get sucked into the evil logic. The one manager who had the most stress that year had to be physically restrained by the rest of the managers at one point so he wouldn't harm the exec. The exec told the manager he wouldn't report the attack. He was so "magnanimous"!

During his year as branch manager, the exec had used all the nasty tactics including embarrassing managers in front of others, shaming them, instilling fear of job loss, and the worst one—boggling the mind. This boss was so good at twisting things that he could make a success look like a failure.

In Chapter 2 we'll look at nasty personalities of bosses, and they don't all seem nasty at first glance. Our obvious archetype nasty boss has more subtle contemporaries. The devil doesn't always look like the devil. Maybe some of these subtler versions are not totally nasty but have some personality traits you need to watch out for. I'll introduce you to the Carrot Dangler, who always wants you to do that one more thing for the promotion and then, oops, just one more. You'll meet the Violator, who gets off on victimizing you. You don't see it coming because you can't conceive of that kind of mentality. The Noper says nope to your ideas, and then later something gets implemented that sure seems like what you suggested. The Chucky Boss uses you and then chucks you in the "wasted" can. Remember that kid who bullied you in school and took your lunch money? He is now the Invalidator. Some of these bosses we can deal with, and others need to become history so we can continue on in our careers. Not only will you meet these and other nasty bosses in this book but I'll tell you how to deal with them—without stooping to their level.

Finally, I want you to be in your prefrontal lobe when you are finished. I want you to see the bigger picture of things, learn to recognize patterns and themes. I want you to exercise that PFL and your executive functions.

NASTY BOSSES

THE GOOD BOSS

In order to define the nasty boss, we almost have to contrast with a good boss, and vice versa. First, let's look at a chart of nasty qualities and the contrasting good qualities. Don't forget, real life won't be as black and white as this. These are polarized models.

Nasty Boss	**Good Boss**
Dominates	Encourages
Blames others	Shares responsibility
Alienates	Welcomes
Hovers	Shows interest
Intimidates	Makes people feel at ease
Instills fear	Instills confidence
Speaks—doesn't listen	Listens
Threatens	Protects

Is egotistical	Has good self-esteem
Is arrogant	Shows humility
Has sense of entitlement	Has sense of purpose
Commands fear	Commands respect
May be intelligent, not wise	Is wise
Only sees what he or she wants	Sees the overall picture
Introverts people with self-doubt	Brings out the best in people
Disrespects	Respects

Charisma

Good bosses will have the ability to connect with people, acknowledge people, and admire people. These three qualities are the secrets of charisma.

Connecting with people includes simply touching them, shaking hands, smiling, looking into their eyes directly.

Acknowledging people means showing a genuine interest in them, realizing their feelings, and understanding their thoughts. You don't have to agree with their thoughts, just understand them. You give empathetic feedback on their feelings.

Admiring people means looking for and verbalizing the good qualities in them. People want to know that you "see" them. See the glass half full instead of half empty.

Good bosses respect others, not because of who the others are, but because of who they themselves are. By the same token, good bosses do not tolerate disrespect from others. Good bosses are not codependent and do not set out for everyone to like them (even though most people do end up liking them).

Good bosses could probably tell you that you need to go to hell in such a way that you would be happy to make the journey (but would probably not do that to you).

Now let's take a longer look at the many types of nasty bosses.

TYPES OF
NASTY BOSSES

There are many types of nasty bosses. I have extracted some traits of nasty bosses from the *DSM-IV*, which is considered the mental health workers' bible. A nasty boss may have some sort of personality disorder or psychological disorder. But some bosses are just selfish, manipulative, degenerate, and/or greedy people. This book is about them. Sometimes there's nothing psychological about it; they just choose to be that way out of selfishness or lack of concern about others.

One type of personality disorder is the antisocial personality disorder (previously called sociopath or psychopath). Probably only about 1 percent of bosses are antisocial. These are bosses with no conscience and no concern for other people. Many other bosses may have features of the antisocial personality but may not be fully diagnosable. The term "antisocial" does not mean that they shy from people. They could be very gregarious and fun-loving. They might enjoy being with people; they just don't give a damn about anyone except themselves.

A psychological disorder might be something like the intermittent explosive disorder. People with an intermittent explosive disorder could actually be bipolar or have had a head injury earlier in life. These people could use an anger management seminar, but they may have a chemical or physiological problem. Bipolar disorder is chemical and hereditary, in which case those who have it can't always help it. Depending on the degree of anger-mania, they may be only partially in control. When people become angry-manic, they have very little prefrontal lobe activity, so they are not seeing themselves in context of the big picture, and their brain is directly connected to their tongue. The best you can do is to not take whatever they say to you personally and just wait until they are in a better mood because they are having mood swings. When their PFL comes back, they may even apologize for what they said. Don't be smug. We all lose our prefrontal lobe capability at times (and some of us don't use it at all, anyway).

So, I have categorized the types using characteristics from the *DSM-IV*, other books, executive interviews, and my own experiences in management.

The Carrot Dangler

The Carrot Dangler waves that raise or promotion in front of you and tells you if you work a little harder or complete a certain project, it is yours. He doesn't promise it but insinuates it. Every time you get close, he "raises the bar" and tells you that you need to jump just a little higher. It is always just one more task.

What do you do? Get it in writing. Pin him down to a more concrete understanding. His PFL is working, but his motives are cat-and-mouse motives.

The Two-Face

The Two-Face tells you one thing, your peers another, and her boss still another. She is a deceptive people pleaser who ends up letting you down and ultimately not pleasing you. In actuality, she doesn't care about pleasing you as much as leading you on. She doesn't like to be confrontational, so you never know if she is being honest or not. She seems "nice," but she is not. It would be better to have a boss who is more direct and honest.

Confront her with "just the facts" (e.g., "You told me I was in a good position to be promoted. You said that your boss really liked me. When I said hello to her today in the hallway and introduced myself, she had no idea who I was.")

The Peoplesuck Boss

The Peoplesuck Boss dislikes people in general. It's too bad he needs them to do the work. He may confide in you how other people suck. He also confides in them about how you suck. It is all a big smoke screen designed to hide the person who really sucks: himself.

Let him know that you do not like to hear negative things about other people. He will stop talking to you so much, but he will have respect for you. He will still talk behind your back, but you haven't lost anything. He was going to do that anyway. Except now he trusts you a little because he knows you are not talking behind his back.

The Crusader

The Crusader is devoted to the cause and the purpose. She expects everyone else to be just as devoted. She will go to any lengths for the client. She "shoulds" all over her staff and expects you to work as hard as she does (for less compensation). Your raise will be denied because it would take away from the profit or would deprive the client of services. Don't try to keep up with her. If you do, she will respect you for a while, until you call in sick one day with double pneumonia from overwork. Then she will feel betrayed by you. Obviously to her, you don't care. She will stay at the Hyatt on a business trip because she is the Crusader, but she'll want you to stay at the Super 8, and she will have surf and turf to keep up her energy, but she'll expect you to grab a fast-food burger. Your indulgence would be taking away from the profits or the client. And what do you mean, your son has a Little League game? You haven't finished your work that she is not paying you overtime for! After all, you are dispensable. Only she is indispensable.

So what do you do? Make her dispensable and find another boss. Her grandiosity and sense of entitlement won't change. Find a boss who is less entitled and more fair. And (P.S.) read *Codependent No More*.

The Chucky Boss

The Chucky Boss has some antisocial features. He doesn't have much of a conscience, and he is not grateful or loyal no matter what you do for him. You will see the trilogy in him (ego, arrogance, entitlement). He could be a good ol' boy and seem to be affectionate at times. He may find your plight amusing but does not have one ounce of empathy. He has a con-artist type of charisma. When he is done using you, he will chuck you in the "wasted" can.

What to do? Don't assume any good graces or long-term relationship with him. Strike your deal, get your compensation up front, and it may work out. Otherwise, don't fall for any of the type of charm he may send your way. If you continue to work for Chucky, you will eventually have a "salmon day." That is the experience of swimming upstream for a long time only to get screwed and die off at the end.

The Enmesher

The Enmesher wants to know all about your private life. Her limits and boundaries are not clear. She may do things like have an affair with someone who works for her. She may want to be your friend, family, and boss all at the same time. She is not inherently nasty, but you may be affected by her life being a wreck. She can be inappropriate and leave you feeling strange. She may tell you that you need to take a business trip with her and the hotel has only one room available so you'll have to share. She may ask you to help with her income taxes—on company time.

Even though she doesn't have limits and boundaries, you can. Do what is appropriate for yourself. Her character is usually not one of vindictiveness. She won't hold it against you if you decline. If you are the type of person who can't say no, read *Codependent No More*.

The Violator

The Violator thrives on stepping over people's boundaries. If he were a woman, he would be a misandrist (woman who hates men) and use psychological castration. For example, if a male employee told his female boss that he would be in late for a 7:00 A.M. meeting because his wife didn't get off work until then, she would respond, "I think you have to decide who wears the pants in your family."

He is probably the reason for the need to pass laws concerning sexual harassment. Most sexual harassment isn't even sexual—it's about domination. Ever see a dog lift its leg and urinate on another dog? Watch this boss in action; it's the same dynamics in play. He could be a misogynist (man who hates women) or just someone who wants to dominate and invalidate no matter what sex the person is— an equal-opportunity victimizer. The misandrist and misogynist are rapists. They mentally rape others and boggle the mind. These people can be so malevolent in a subtle way that they get away with ruining a person with no consequences to themselves.

What do you do with people who like to dominate in this manner? One thing that would work is for you to dominate them. If they are bosses, that is going to be hard. If they have a dominating personality, they are probably better at it than you are. One approach that may work is to privately let them know that you like them but you know what they're doing. Publicly, let them be dominant over you if you can, while giving them a knowing smile. They may respect you and then go after easier prey. Bullies like easier prey.

Another thing you can do is document all your interactions with Violators over a period of time and show it to one of their superiors. Be sure to note the mind-boggling interactions (mental rape). If it gets bad, find another job.

The Invalidator

The Invalidator is good at making you feel as big as the period at the end of this sentence. She is different from the Violator; she may use similar tactics, but her intent is not to victimize you so much as it is to defend herself. You will see the trilogy (ego, arrogance, entitlement), especially when she feels threatened. Perhaps there was a victimizer in her past. She is a bully sometimes. She was the bully in school that got all of her friends to turn against a girl that she didn't like. She is liable to use intimidation, fear, and threats when she feels backed into a corner. She always has to be "right" and "win." She may not be out to dominate but may feel as if she has to dominate or be dominated. She doesn't want to be the victim, so she overcompensates.

So, what is going to work with her? Ready for this? . . . *Nurturing.* Huh!? It may be the very last thing you feel like doing, yet that's what will work. You can always spot bullies: they're the ones who haven't been nurtured. Of course, you can't nurture her in a condescending manner. You must do so in appropriate ways. Smile at her. Like her. Respect her. Never embarrass her in front of others. Notice her good qualities. Keep doing this until she feels safe with you. Keep doing this until she values you, and she will, because she needs that nurturing. She is not going to hurt the one who nurtures her. In *Anger Kills*, research showed that one of the most important causes of hostility is a lack of nurturing. Where you have a lack of nurturing, you have a lack of self-esteem. Where you have a lack of self-esteem, you have a preponderance of ego. There is a big difference between self-esteem and ego. Ego is just a smoke screen hiding a lack of self-esteem. Nurturing is what gives us good self-esteem; hostility is, therefore, from a lack of nurturing.

The Invalidator's inner child has been damaged. Treat her accordingly and with respect. Manage your manager.

An alternative I do not recommend would be to give her back the abuse she gives you. You could raise your voice to her in the office. Make a scene, yell at her, and draw attention. This may give you some satisfaction after you are outside the facility looking for another job.

The Noper

The Noper always says no to your ideas, but then you notice that they get implemented as *his* ideas!

The solution is simple. When you have an idea, send him a memo—put it in writing. I found that I could get to do what *I* wanted to do in my corporate world as long as I didn't care who got credit for the idea. With my psychology training, I would go to meetings and ask just the right questions until someone else had the idea. I remember an executive coming up to me once and saying, "Well, you don't contribute that much to the meetings, but I am leaving you on the list and we still would like to have you come." It showed that he had some very small bit of insight. It's amazing how much you can get done if you don't need credit for it.

The Anal-izer

The Anal-izer does not have an operational prefrontal lobe. She has little insight, foresight, or vision. This person does not sit in the captain's chair because she is too busy down below making sure everyone is doing their jobs the way she wants them to. She has problems delegating. If she had her way, she would do everything herself. She is very moral and "righteous." And "right" means "her way." She is not very personable, and she believes that people (even herself) do not live up to what they are supposed to do. She is proper (or, as they say in England, "propah"). She may appear to be snooty, judgmental, and arrogant. She doesn't have enough self-esteem or ego to be snooty, but she is very opinionated. She is not actually arrogant, but she is judgmental. She is a workaholic. She spends a lot of time attending to details, but she doesn't see the big picture. You may have met a teacher like her in school. After you wrote a brilliant essay, she gave you a D because it wasn't typewritten. Remember her?

What to do? First, don't take it personally. It isn't. She treats everyone like that, even herself. She is not going to think out of the box, and you won't get your raise or promotion early no matter what you do, but you will get it at the "propah" time.

The MeMe Boss

Everything relates to him. If you make a mistake, he says, "How could you do that . . . *to me*?" If something goes well for him, he thinks he is the greatest and the whole world revolves around him. If he messes up, he feels as if he is a piece of junk—that the whole world revolves around. Don't ever forget MeMe's birthday. He can be vindictive and vengeful. He may pout. If his department misses a deadline, he can't understand it ("I thought you all liked me!"). He feels entitled to all the adoration and credit he thinks he deserves. The technical term for him is *narcissist*. That doesn't make him a bad person. He may be a good narcissist. That means that he will fight to get you that gold pen, because if he were you, he would really want it badly. He really thinks he is *it* and will not be willing to entertain ideas that he needs improvement or that he made a mistake. He sports the trilogy (ego, arrogance, entitlement), although not so malevolently and uncaringly as some of his counterparts. He will show empathy if he ever went through the same thing you are going through. He will help you the way he wanted help when that happened to him. If you are lucky, it may be a match.

If you can work with him and make him feel you admire him, things may be fine. He may shower you with benevolence as long as you don't appear to take away the attention he may get from others. As long as you uphold him as higher than yourself, he will let you have some of the fame and fortune. He takes everything personally, though, so watch your step.

The Mood

Every day you wonder what mood she is going to be in. If she is in a good mood, you get to be an exemplary employee. If she is in a bad mood, you might get written up. In a good mood she remembers all the wonderful things you have done. In a bad mood she remembers all the times you messed up. If your appraisal comes on a bad-mood day, go home sick and postpone it. She will think you are a dirtball, but she is going to think that anyway on that day.

Sometimes her PFL is operating. She is able to see the big picture. Other days, she is all black and white and strict rules govern the day. Sometimes it seems that she sabotages projects right at the end. She dramatizes things with anger and sometimes with that sad inner-child look. It almost seems as if she creates the drama. Sometimes you feel like a pawn in whatever game she is playing, but you can't figure out what her purpose is.

If it "seems" that she is sabotaging, she is. If it "seems" that she is dramatizing, she is. If you can't figure out what purpose she has, she probably doesn't have one. She doesn't know why she does these things either. She could be bipolar and having mood swings, or she could be a borderline personality who gets set off by relationship cues. She may not realize she is sabotaging or dramatizing. She doesn't "see herself" during these times. There is no PFL working. She may have a history of her employees bailing her out of these moods. They throw themselves on the railroad tracks in front of her oncoming mood. She may or may not appreciate it later.

If you work for her, you may end up with a lot of anxiety due to the unpredictability that exudes from her persona. At times she may be generous and put you on a pedestal. But you will have to assess how many times you can let her mood train pass over your psyche on the railroad tracks of your work life. If you can deal with the uncertainty and you are also able to *not* take it personally, you may be all right. If not, you may have to find a new boss.

"Nasty" Female Bosses

Due to popular request I am including a section specifically on nasty female bosses—not as a type of boss, but because there is a large misunderstanding of gender-specific behavior, and the approach of a female boss is usually different from that of a male boss. So I hope this section also corrects misunderstandings about female bosses who may not actually be nasty.

Most of the time, the perception of "someone of gender" being "nasty" is a misunderstanding. Men and women are far more different from each other than we ever thought. And women are far more powerful than they think. In management, the power of a woman does not lie in how much a woman can act like a man. This is a mistake that some women make in management. For example, in our society, when a man is angry, he is seen as "being assertive." When a woman is angry she is seen as "being a bitch." When a woman tries to act like a man using anger to make a point, she may notice it doesn't have the effect that she wants so she overcompensates by turning up the intensity. That is usually perceived by men as going from bitchy to demented. The respect is diminished. The result is not what she wanted.

Please allow me to generalize a bit. I realize I am generalizing. A man perceives his power as what he *does*. His accomplishments give him his confidence and his esteem. A woman's power lies in her *being*—who she *is*.

Women have shaped our civilization for thousands of years. The hand that rocks the cradle has been a subtle but powerful influence. There is an ancient (3,800-year-old) phrase documented in the Old Testament: "A man cleaves to his mother, then he leaves his mother and cleaves to his wife." This is not so much a religious statement as it is the documentation of a process. I never really understood it until recently. How would I stop "cleaving" if I wanted to, and how would I start "cleaving" if I wanted to? But the meaning of this ancient knowledge is the secret to the influence women have and to their success, if they use it.

Bear with me. I am getting to the point here, but it is a "big picture" thought, not just one small detail. It requires the engagement of executive functions in the prefrontal lobes to be understood.

Freud missed this one, perhaps because he was so male-oriented. Who influences a boy most during the first five years of his life (his most crucial development)? Yes, his mother. So where does he get his self-esteem? From a woman. When a man deals with a woman later in his life— whether she is his boss or his significant other—he allows his self-esteem to be more vulnerable by putting it in her hands. He does this unconsciously. She becomes significant to him and what she thinks of him becomes very important to him, even though she is not completely aware this is going on in his mind and emotions.

To the Female Boss of a Male Employee

In management, we all know that people react to their bosses in some ways as they have reacted to other authority figures in their life. Ah—so it becomes very important to a man what his female boss thinks of him. His relationship with her has an impact on his self-esteem. Who she is becomes important to him—not to say she should inappropriately take on a mother role, but she should command respect in the appropriate situations (e.g., evaluations). Trying to please her or appease her may not work out well, but she can motivate him to live up to an *image* that she has of him (her expectations).

It is a well-known management technique to say something good about an employee before something negative. That is only *part* of the technique. After a while employees catch on and give you the hairy eyeball when you say something good about them . . . waiting for the negative punch line. The more effective and complete way is to paint the bigger positive picture of a person before taking him to task for some mistake he may have made. If someone loses money for the organization because of something he has done, you shouldn't bring him in the office and immediately ream him out ("I can't believe you lost us one thousand dollars! You are so irresponsible! How could you be that careless!?"). That leaves him wondering if he should look for another job. His boss is upset and she thinks he is careless and irresponsible. The esteem hurts. It brings him into a sort of apathy because he can't undo the past. This is important for any boss to know, but especially important for a female boss and male employee.

A better approach is to invoke the executive function and look at the bigger picture. That conversation may go like this: "I see you have been working for us for ten years. You have received five awards. You have hardly any sick time off. You are a good employee." That paints the foreground. Now you take him to task and get your feelings out: "That's why I can't understand how you could do something that irresponsible and careless!!!" You see, now he knows he is held in high esteem. Men are word-oriented and take words literally and generally (I am generalizing, of course). Once you give the bigger picture of him (he is not generally irresponsible and careless), you have painted an image for him to live up to. Now he is not apathetic; he is motivated to live up to that image. He walks out of the office feeling ready to do better—knowing that he can and that this woman has faith in him. Therein lies the power of a woman.

Women are perceived as being nasty when they try to act like men. They are even perceived as being nasty when they try to get a man to live up to his potential. One sees this in a marriage where a woman marries a man for his potential and then proceeds to make him her "home improvement project." This goes on in the workplace as well. A man may perceive his boss as "dissatisfied," "nagging," and "complaining" and may feel he can never please her. She is just trying to get him to be the man/employee that she knows he can be. She is showing faith in him. But men like acceptance to a fault. He feels she doesn't accept him for who he is. Again, painting the foreground for how generally competent he is will allow him to see the defect that taints his image (which is actually her image of him).

Male bosses usually have more concern about deadlines and less concern about maintaining a relationship. In a long-term business relationship, the employee builds resentment for this type of boss because the deadline always comes first no matter what hardship it causes. The corporate world recognized a "problem" with long-term management relationships (although they couldn't identify it) and began switching management every few years to deal with employee dissatisfaction. Women in management seem to be able to maintain business relationships more productively over the long term. It seems that women are more forgiving and less vengeful than men in the business world in many ways. Women also tend to do the maintenance that relationships require (venting to clear the air, *not* harboring resentment, etc.). Male employees care about what a male boss thinks of their abilities, but they are concerned with what a female boss thinks of them personally.

One more interesting aside that I have found: women do not appreciate name-calling and usually don't put up with it. If a woman is called "bitch," she doesn't like it. Men can be called a jerk, an ass, and other names without getting so upset. Name-calling to a man is when you call him "immature," "irresponsible," "ignorant," or any of those types of names. If you call a woman "irresponsible," she is liable to not take it so personally and to ask, "Why, what did I do?" If you call a man "irresponsible," he is liable to give a long defensive philosophical argument about how you are wrong and examples of his most responsible achievements. He may be so busy defending himself, he may not realize that you are just upset with him. Men take words literally and generally and as attacks on esteem, whereas women usually mean them specifically and aimed at a behavior rather than as a general shot to the esteem. If you call a man a jerk, he may not take it so personally and ask, "Why, what did I do?" He just figures you are upset about something, and he doesn't think you are so nasty. Being a "jerk" is not as degrading to a man as being "irresponsible."

Men get angry when you have hurt their feelings. And men's feelings are hurt when they feel an attack on their esteem. That doesn't mean that one should stroke the ego. There is a big difference between ego and self-esteem. Stroking self-esteem is when you mention things that already are good qualities (e.g., loyal, kind, compassionate, dedicated). Stroking ego is when you make a big fuss about the gold chain, big car, or prowess. A man knows the difference.

If you want to make a man live up to his potential, you cannot help him do it without stroking his self-esteem. If you don't remind him of his good qualities, he will take the "suggestions for improvement" as nagging, complaining, and your dissatisfaction with him. He will see you as a nasty woman. If you don't want to stroke his inner child and you think that you shouldn't have to do that, then you must also give up on trying to improve him and just accept him the way he is.

Mothers are of tantamount importance to a man. Just before their execution, many inmates call out for their mothers. If Attila the Hun was having a board meeting and his mother walked in, he might say, "How am I doing, Mum?"

Men command respect (fear?) by domination. The male executive manager does not necessarily get his position by how fair or reasonable he is but by what he has accomplished and his leadership (domination ability). This may work for some women over some men, but generally a woman gets her power in his perception by her supervisory position, from the bond she develops with him (by being someone he wants to work with), and by being someone whose perception he values. Concretely, she becomes an authority figure by:

1. Being in a more powerful position (she is the boss)
2. Putting him in a good light (whenever she can)
3. Liking him, or if that's not possible, respecting him
4. Admiring him (it must be genuine)

Sometimes it's hard to respect someone, so you may have to ask yourself, "Do I respect people because of who *they* are or because of who *I* am?" Sometimes it's hard to find something genuine to admire about someone. What do you admire about a drug dealer ("I like your gold chain")?

To the Female Boss of a Female Employee

This is going to be a much more concise section than the previous (more difficult) one. It's shorter but poignant, so pay attention. Do unto others as you would have them do unto you, if they were *your* boss.

THE THREE MENTALITIES

This "practical psychology minicourse" is going to provide the basis for understanding your boss (or yourself or anyone else) in a unique way that will give you an edge and will be very much worth your while. With this background, a more lengthy explanation will not be necessary and you will have a feel for what is going on with your boss. Developing an awareness leads to concrete methods. So bear with me . . . unless you want to do this book *your way*, in which case you should just put this book down right now and go back to doing things *your way*. To understand people and to understand your boss, we need to talk about the three mentalities. We are all born with a certain temperament (mammal), cognitive ability (logic), and long-range awareness (executive functions/prefrontal lobe). To understand your boss (and yourself) it helps to know his or her temperament, cognitive ability, and level of awareness. If you have a collie temperament and your boss has a pit bull temperament, it is going to be beneficial to understand that. This chapter contains some major secrets to success. You won't be stuck with just the verbal world of communication. You will be able to decipher the nonverbal and intuitive levels. You can discover the secret to unlocking your own true charisma. You can develop your instincts and your intuition. If your boss is an undisciplined pit bull, doesn't see the big picture of anything, and has a prime instinct to dominate you, it is probably not going to behoove you to work for him or her. If you could see that up front before you wasted six months working for him or her, you might be all the better for it. If your boss has a collie mentality but is a procrastinator and never stands up for your promotions or raises, you also might like to see that coming before you waste six months. You might even find some things about yourself that you didn't realize you could improve. I think you will find this chapter interesting, enlightening, and useful.

Let's start with the mentality we are born with—the mammal mentality that is forged in our genes from millions of years of existence and is programmed for survival.

The Mammal Mentality

The way a mammal "thinks" is simply by association. You say "sit," and your mammal sits. It doesn't form full sentences or have rules. It operates on the stimulus-response mechanism and preprogrammed instincts just like all other mammals. It is not that bright, but it is usually cooperative. Right now, your mammal is moving its eyes across the page because you are directing it to. It is usually obedient to simple commands. My mammal is actually a he rather than an it. He is usually obedient except when I walk down the candy aisle in the supermarket. If I do, he will go get a bag of chocolate! He doesn't care about how well I have been doing on my diet or anything else. He feels guilty when I scold him for eating the chocolate but not guilty enough to stop. If I don't walk him down the candy aisle, he doesn't misbehave like that . . . unless I fantasize about chocolate and get him all worked up. Then he finds the candy aisle like a mouse finds the cheese in a maze. He usually reacts only to what is in front of him at any given moment. Most of us can be cognitively philosophical about going on a diet, but put a piece of chocolate in front of our mammals and watch out.

The Cognitive Mentality

Our cognitive mentality (logic) starts developing early but is not mature enough for use until we are about five (for some, three and for others, eight). When you begin to call yourself "I," it signifies the basic finished development of the cognitive mentality. We begin to have a consistent cognitive memory then. Prior to that we remember only in pictures (the movie film memory). We are trained to use our cognitive memory more and more as we attend school, and most of us operate the moving picture memory less and less.

This cognitive mentality forms full sentences. It is what you are reading this sentence with right now. It enables you to do mathematical problems. It allows you to form beliefs. These beliefs come to us (as "downloads") from our parents, culture, community, school, and church. By the time we are ten years old, we operate like beings that are two hundred years old. Think about it—all that culture and language. We absorb and remember so much information because as children we don't challenge any of it. We accept everything that we hear and see. Everything we are told gets downloaded into the cognitive memory banks. And we do accept it, because we have no perspective on it yet. We don't get perspective until the prefrontal lobe kicks in. The prefrontal lobe is the most sophisticated mentality of the human race.

The Prefrontal Lobe Mentality

Out of the prefrontal lobe comes the highest mentality in the human being. It's the part of you that sees the bigger picture. It is the captain's chair of your mentality. It is that part of your mentality that views via 360 degrees of windows of the mind, so you can see where you are going, where you have been, and whether anything is coming in from the sides. Research says that the prefrontal lobe continues to develop into the late thirties.

Some people have prefrontal lobe difficulties in that they are not able to see the big picture of things or assess the consequences of their actions. These are people who might be diagnosed with attention deficit disorder (ADD), attention deficit/hyperactivity disorder (ADHD), developmental problems, or learning disorders. Note, however, that not all people with these types of problems have a prefrontal lobe difficulty. That's why I want to call it "prefrontal lobe difficulty" instead of ADD, ADHD, etc. The ones who do have these problems may benefit from some of the newer nontoxic, nonaddictive remedies such as Wellbutrin or Strattera.

The prefrontal lobe is literally what separates us from the animals. Usually we start looking at our beliefs after the prefrontal lobe kicks in. That's when we say things like, "Mom, *why* is it bad for me to have sex even if I use birth control?" Until then, we operate purely according to the rules. Everything is black and white before then. When we get perspective, we start questioning things. That's when "Because I said so . . ." is no longer valid. Life is still simple though. If the neighbor is having a problem with alcoholism, the newly developed prefrontal lobe candidate will say, "Simple. He just has to stop drinking." In our infancy of perspective, we may have such simple solutions for things.

Once our brain develops the prefrontal lobe capability, we are able to "see ourselves" in perspective with others. We get the ability to put ourselves in another's place and try to imagine what that person must feel like. We direct our imagination to calculate the consequences of what we do.

How the Three Mentalities Work Together

So if we can be aware of our cognitive thinking and we can be aware of the mammal part of us, what is that? That is being *aware* of these two mentalities. Our human mammal has an awareness just like any other animal. And we are aware of our thinking. We know when we are thinking and what we are thinking about. The part of us that *sees* our mammal reactions and *sees* our thoughts is the prefrontal lobe. It is the self-awareness that we have that other animals don't have. This is the part that is the boss of ourselves. It is the part that sees things coming and invokes the mammal and cognitive mentalities strategically.

People with good cognitive mentality can get straight As in school. These people might be able to get a 4.0 in an engineering program, but without the PFL to apply what they learned, they may never be able to build bridges. With a good set of rules or objectives, these people can accomplish quite a bit. They may be able to be expert programmers, but without the PFL, their work may not be very "user-friendly" because they won't be able to see or project the environment of the users. We don't need to say much more about the cognitive mentality (the part that's reading this paragraph right now).

In our society, we worship the "cognitive god." Everyone wants their children to go to college . . . so that they can make less money than a plumber. Why? I don't know. Some people cannot stand to go to school. They are not cognitively oriented. If they had to attend a lecture on "How to Fix a Kitchen Sink," they would fidget and be unable to pay attention. If you *showed* these same people how to fix a kitchen sink they might be able to do it right from that moment on. People learn in different ways and it doesn't have to be cognitively. Some people are more physically oriented (sight, sound, touch) and not so "thinking" oriented. There is nothing wrong with this. It doesn't mean that they have less of a PFL. The PFL is an awareness, not a thought process. I am always amazed at the PFL awareness of some people with Down syndrome. They can be so aware of other people's feelings, far beyond the capability that some of us scholars have. They may not have the cognitive ability, but their PFL and their mammal mentality function just fine. If your boss doesn't use the PFL and you do, you can be an asset to the boss. Not all bosses use the PFL, but some of them have good enough instincts to hire people who do have a good PFL. This boss might be a good opportunist and a good person to deal with emergencies but may need direction from you (in a respectful, suggestive, nonthreatening way). If you find yourself in the position of providing your PFL to the boss, make sure you get paid for it. Make sure you get treated well for your insights. Make sure you don't get dominated to the point of suppression or oppression. If the boss does have good instincts, he or she will know your worth. If that's not the case, find a new boss.

The Processors Interact to Create Balance

The human mammal mentality processes feelings and instincts and senses danger. The processors interact as shown here:

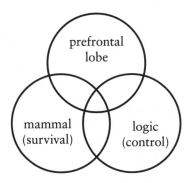

These processors interact with each other directly and indirectly. The mammal has been programmed for millions upon millions of years through genetics to survive. It has developed intuition and instinct, and it can sense immediate danger. It is not very bright, logically speaking. It can't form sentences. It has no idea what I am saying. It is just moving its eyes across the page as you command it to. For the most part, it is very cooperative and does what you direct it to do.

The logic (cognitive) processor interprets what is being said here. It hasn't been around as long as the mammal processor (possibly only a million years). It is programmed to be in control. It has refined its logic over the generations. It can anticipate things it has repeated habitually in the past. It can form full thoughts.

Generally, the processors work together to create a balance in our lives. Most of the time the mammal obeys the logic or PFL and takes over only when survival is at stake or a pleasure moment is forthcoming. The mammal is usually very loyal and obedient. It learns by association. You say "sit" and it sits. Of course, you don't even have to say "sit," because the mammal is hooked up telepathically. I am going to call the mammal "it" for descriptive purposes, but the mammal is actually a he or she. The mammal is similar to a gorilla in function but like a dog in mentality. It has a wide range of associative abilities. Whereas a gorilla may be able to associate only two hundred words to objects, the human mammal can associate thousands. The mammal holds the experiential memories (our experiences), including perceptions and feelings. The mammal operates in the now. It is eternally present. If the mammal has a memory of being hit by a baseball bat, the presence of a baseball bat may cause it to have a negative reaction. The mammal cannot anticipate the future except through stimulus response, moving picture memories from the past, and genetically programmed reactions. Even then, it only reacts out of stimulus response.

The logic (cognitive function) is the rational function. It is also in the eternal present but can be influenced by the mammal's reaction to past memories and by anticipating the future (via PFL imagination). Some say the rational part of man is a part of the brain no bigger than a walnut. It begins behind the PFL but pervades the brain. If we rolled it up, it may be the size of a walnut. The mammal cannot be defined in a particular part of the brain either, as it seems to pervade it, but it is somewhere in the back of the skull. The mammal and logic are *functions* of the mind, and we are not going to waste time trying to define their exact organic locations. The logic contains the rules of the culture, family, religion, and society passed down in the form of "beliefs" and holds all our beliefs, including the "shoulds." We know what we should do, but we don't do what we should sometimes. Then, afterward, we usually guilt ourselves with "should haves." Why don't we do what we should do? Many of us have come to know that we have some sort of addiction, whether it is drugs, alcohol, work, obsessions, or chocolate. The mammal works on the pleasure/pain stimulus-response principle. Let me tell you a little story about the mentalities and alcoholism, which may seem unrelated to nasty bosses but is necessary to give you a feel for the human mammal that you wouldn't otherwise have.

The Alcoholic

An alcoholic goes to a rehab for twenty-eight days. At the time of discharge, there is no desire to have a drink. The mammal doesn't have much of a memory—only the picture memory, which activates a mammal by association. The mammal has been away from alcohol for twenty-eight days. The logic has been trained and educated in the downfalls of alcoholism. On the way home, our alcoholic has a fleeting thought: "Maybe I shouldn't drive by the bar I used to go to." The logic (which doesn't have a good understanding of the mammal) says, "That's stupid. Heck, I don't even *feel* like having a drink. I'll be OK." So, the alcoholic drives by the bar and the mammal *sees the sign*. The logic has a thought: "Gee, maybe I should stop to see my friends. I won't drink anything." The alcoholic parks the car and walks up to the door. As the door opens, the mammal *smells the beer*. Now the mammal has *seen the sign* and *smelled the beer*. The alcoholic says hello to his buddies, and one of them says, "Hey. You're cured now. Have a beer! It won't hurt you to have one beer!" Our alcoholic's logic says to itself, "I'll have *one* beer. This will be the last beer I ever have in my life." So, the alcoholic has a beer. Now the mammal has *seen the sign*, *smelled the beer*, and *tasted the beer*. Is he going to have another beer? Oh, yes. And this time he is going to rationalize, "Well, I can have one more beer and still be under the legal limit for a DUI, and *this* will be the last beer I ever have in my life." Now the mammal has *seen the sign*, *smelled the beer*, *tasted the beer*, and is *under the influence of two beers*. Is he going to have another beer? You betcha! And this time he is going to rationalize, "Well, heck, I blew it now. I might as well tie one on, but this will be the last time I ever do it in my whole life."

Is he going to come back to the bar again? Oh, yes.

Alcoholism is a very good illustration of the conflict between the mammal and the logic. "What conflictt? Thersh no conflictt!"

There are so many of us who have addictions to things like drugs, alcohol, food, sex, work, and money that it would be helpful if we understood the mammal/logic process. Of course, the only one that *understands* things is the logical processor. The biological processor (mammal) just *reacts* to things. The logical processor may identify some of these addictions by adding a judgmental quality to it (gluttony, lust, greed, etc.).

Back to the Mammal

Let's return to the mammal mentality and how it applies to bosses. No matter how smart we are, cognitively, and no matter how much we are able to see the big picture of things, we are still mammals. We don't like to think of ourselves as mammals, but we all have different temperaments. We are different sexes. The mammal is a he or a she. Realistically, we have to take your boss's mammal into consideration. There are many different temperaments. Is your boss a collie temperament, or German shepherd, or pit bull, or shih tzu? If you abuse a collie, it will avoid you. If you abuse a German shepherd, it may bite you. If you abuse a pit bull, it may kill you. If you abuse a shih tzu, it will still like you (and maybe even become your therapist). If you have more than one child, are they the same? Most likely not. You can't raise a pit bull the same way you raise a collie. A pit bull boss with a good PFL disciplines the mammal well and looks at what she or he is about to say before spitting it out. Psychology skirts the issue of temperament because it's not "scientific," so when your undisciplined pit bull boss is growling at you, psychology doesn't know what to tell you . . . scientifically speaking.

I do. If your pit bull boss is looking at you with blank eyes and is making hostile gestures . . . *run*! A surge of adrenaline takes twelve to twenty minutes to run through a human being. During that time the body uses all the lactose in the muscles and all the glucose in the veins. After that twelve to twenty minutes, the person becomes physically depressed. So when your boss gets a surge of adrenaline, find someplace to hide for a while. After that, seek the boss out during the physical depression, when he or she will be more agreeable.

Back in the day when hitting your kid was not considered physical abuse, I remember incidents with my father where he would be upset about something and work himself up to an angry state where he would give us a spanking. During that time I would sit there and listen . . . knowing it was coming. My youngest brother was smarter than the rest of us. He would run. He was driving along with my father in his pickup truck one day, and my father was upset because my brother had forgotten to feed and water a cow and the cow lost weight and had become dehydrated. My father started to get himself worked up, and my brother knew he was going to get a spanking. So, at the next stop sign, my brother jumped out of the truck and started running through a cornfield. This enraged my father and my father chased after him, growling and barking (not literally). After twelve to twenty minutes, my father seemed exhausted and asked my brother to get back in the truck. My brother asked if he was going to get a spanking. My father sighed, "No, just get back in the truck." My brother had more knowledge about the human mammal than most of us do (even though he dehydrated a cow).

In order to truly understand the mammal mentality (and therefore truly understand your boss), I have provided more information here. Read it. You'll be glad you did.

The mammal is one of the keys to understanding the boss's behavior. A boss with a German shepherd temperament is going to be territorial, protective, and loyal but may bite you once in a while without breaking the skin. A pit bull is going to be confrontational, aggressive, and protective and may really hurt you once in a while.

If you had a problem (let's say where you were fearful when you gave presentations), some bosses would be empathetic and try to accommodate you, some would see it as a weakness and lose respect, some would just judge you on how well you did regardless of your emotions, and some would make you give more presentations, mentoring you to get over it. Which one is right for you? Enabling you may ensure that you wimp out all the time. Scaring the heck out of you may make you swim or drown. Each of us has good temperament matches and bad matches. Some of this shows up in divorce statistics, layoffs, personality conflicts, and transfers. Even if your boss can't understand you, you can at least get more understanding of your boss so you don't make any ultimate faux pas. Your boss may have the same temperament as someone from your past, and knowing that would be the first step in dealing with it.

"Who's Driving?"

Having a mammal processor is just like having a loyal dog at your side at all times. A good dog is always with the master, protecting the master, sensing danger for the master. Did you ever nod off while driving? Did something then jerk you awake? That was the mammal, sensing danger. Did you ever get engrossed in a conversation on your cell phone in your car and suddenly become aware of a dangerous situation? The mammal was watching, and it nudged you when it sensed danger. You drop the cell phone and grab the wheel.

We actually teach the mammal how to drive. At first we use our logic to "figure" it out. The gearshift goes here. The wheel turns this way. As we are doing this, the mammal is made to repeat the driving activities over and over again. It learns to drive by association, and it acquires the skill. After the mammal "knows" how to drive, we don't need to *think* about it anymore. Then we can be occupied with other things while the mammal drives. I've seen people phoning, putting on makeup, and even reading while the mammal is driving.

Did you ever get so drunk you couldn't remember driving home, and you wondered how you got home? It was the mammal who drove you home.

Mammal Interactions in the Workplace

I was in the Philippines for a month and didn't speak the language. I am normally a very word-oriented cognitive person, but I had to learn to read people's emotions and physical gestures to help me understand what they were saying. People in the Philippines understand English, but they rarely speak it and are often embarrassed to try. I learned to ignore the words and interpret nonverbal communication. It was an enlightening experience.

When I got back to the United States, I was still in that mode and went to an executive manager's meeting in Purchase, New York. I sat at a conference table with a bunch of directors who were waiting for a new vice president to officiate. I didn't listen to their words and only noticed their mammal interactions. How enlightening it was. I don't mean this derogatorily, but it was analogous to a pack of dogs vying for position to see who would be the alpha leader. They were checking each other out, not by sniffing each other, but by asking questions. Some were verbally trying to dominate each other. Some were showing submission, not by showing their necks, but by letting the others know in subtler ways that they were no threat (agreeing, listening, being unopinionated, etc.). Some, who were vying for position, were verbally urinating on others by directing invalidation, embarrassment, and derogatory jokes at them. Finally, one director (who had a loud bark, had a long string of accomplishments, and had dominated some of the other directors before) seemed to emerge as the alpha personality. You can learn so much from these interactions.

Try this for yourself. Go to a meeting and look at the emotions and the gestures. Try to assess what each person's temperament might be—not by thinking about it, but by *experiencing* that person. Try this exercise again and again until you are able to readily *feel* the presence of another. A good executive has a feel for other people. Develop it in yourself. Most of the time, people get upset with other people because the person hasn't treated their mammal right. You can avoid a lot of mammal problems by learning the nonverbal mammal language.

Assessing Your Boss

The following checklist will help you identify the problem areas and positive areas of dealings with your boss. Each item describes a characteristic of your boss. From the number choices given, write down the one that most closely matches your opinion of whether your boss has that characteristic. The higher the number, the more strongly you agree that your boss has that attribute. If an item doesn't apply to your boss, mark "0." Make sure you fill in the minuses if shown.

Mammal Checklist
_____ Is aggressive *(in a good way: 1, 3, 5; in a bad way:* $-1, -3, -5)$
_____ Needs to dominate *(−1, −3, −5)*
_____ Barks—doesn't listen *(−1, −3, −5)*
_____ Instills fear (vs. respect) *(−1, −3, −5)*

_____ Is nonthreatening *(in a good way: 1, 3, 5;*
in a bad way: −1, −3, −5)

Shows these emotions:

    _____ Is angry *(1, 2, 3, −1, −2, −3)*

    _____ Is fearful *(−1, −2, −3)*

    _____ Is affectionate (toward you) *(3, 5, 7, 10)*

    _____ Shows no emotion *(1, 2, 3, −1, −2, −3)*

    _____ Is anxious *(−1, −2, −3)*

    _____ Is suspicious *(−1, −3, −5)*

_____ Feels entitled inappropriately *(−1, −3, −5)*

_____ Is protective (toward you) *(1, 5, 10, −1, −5, −7)*

_____ Is empathetic (toward you) *(3, 5, 7, 10, −3, −5, −7)*

_____ Is territorial *(1, 2, 3, −1, −2, −3)*

_____ Is charismatic *(3, 5, 7)*

_____ Is able to bond (with you) *(1, 3, 5, 7, 10)*

_____ Alienates *(−1, −3, −5)*

_____ Intimidates *(1, 2, 3, −1, −3, −5)*

_____ Has an attitude that "people suck" *(−1, −3, −5)*

_____ Is moody *(−1, −3, −5)*

_____ Lacks conscience *(−10, −20, −30)*

_____ Is coldly cordial *(−5, −10, −15)*

_____ Has inappropriate boundaries *(−1, −3, −5)*

_____ Degrades/dominates *(−10, −20, −30)*

_____ Is defensive/bullies *(−1, −3, −5)*

Any other mammal traits? Write them in and rate
them:

_____ ____

_____ ____

Add up all the numbers in the mammal section.

Total _____

Compatibility: 40 plus is excellent; 30–39 is good; 0–29 is fair; −1–−20 is poor; below −20 is incompatible.

Cognitive Checklist

_____ Invalidates *(−1, −5, −10)*

_____ Validates *(1, 5, 10)*

_____ Manipulates *(−1, −3, −5)*

_____ Is argumentative *(−1, −3, −5)*

_____ Is dishonest *(−1, −3, −5)*

_____ Listens *(3, 5, 7, 10, −3, −5, −7)*

_____ Is authoritarian (wants you to just do it)
(1, 2, 3, −1, −3, −5)

_____ Is authoritative (wants you to just do it and tells you why) *(1, 3, 5)*

_____ Is permissive (wants you to figure things out)
(1, 2, 3, −1, −2, −3)

_____ Is a mind-boggler *(−5, −10, −15)*

_____ Always has to be "right" *(−1, −3, −5)*

_____ Always has to win *(−1, −3, −5)*

_____ Acknowledges you *(1, 3, 5, 7, 10)*

_____ Blames *(−1, −3, −5)*

_____ Is egotistical *(−1, −3, −5)*

_____ Is arrogant *(−1, −3, −5)*

_____ Has tunnel vision *(−1, −3, −5)*

_____ Is disrespectful *(−1, −3, −5, −7, −10)*

____ Steals/dismisses your ideas *(−1, −3, −5, −7)*
____ Misses the big picture *(−1, −3, −5)*

Any other cognitive traits? Write them in and rate them:

_____ ____
_____ ____

Add up all the numbers in the cognitive section.

Total _____

Compatibility: 30 plus is excellent; 15–29 is good; 0–14 is fair; −1−−20 is poor; below −20 is incompatible.

Prefrontal Lobe (PFL) Checklist
____ Sees the big picture *(1, 5, 10, −1, −5, −10)*
____ Has integrity *(1, 3, 5, −1, −3, −5)*
____ Is fair *(1, 3, 5, −1, −3, −5)*
____ Has good work ethics *(1, 2, 3, −1, −2, −3)*
____ Shows you the big picture *(1, 2, 3, −1, −2, −3)*
____ Is wise *(1, 2, 3, −1, −2, −3)*
____ Has a sense of purpose *(1, 3, 5, −1, −3, −5)*
____ Has vision *(1, 3, 5, −1, −3, −5)*
____ Is unpredictable *(−1, −2, −3)*
____ Holds back/dangles rewards *(−1, −3, −5)*
____ Is two-faced *(−1, −2, −3)*
____ Has high expectations but low rewards *(−1, −3, −5)*

Any other PFL traits? Write them in and rate them:

_____ ____
_____ ____

Add up all the numbers in the PFL section.

Total _____

Compatibility: 30 plus is excellent; 15–29 is good; 1–14 is fair; 0––9 is poor; below −10 is incompatible.

"Excellent" means that you are compatible with your boss in that area. "Good" means that you are compatible, but there is room for improvement. "Fair" means that you can be successful in improving the area of compatibility but it's going to be difficult.

If compatibility is "fair" in the area of the mammal, you should assess your temperament and your boss's temperament. For example, if you are both pit bulls, perhaps you need to submit to your boss (as long as he or she is your boss) and try not to impose yourself on the boss so much. If you are a collie and your boss is a pit bull, perhaps you need to respectfully confront the boss, when appropriate, so the boss has more respect for you. The secret to improving the compatibility of this mentality is to show affinity to the boss. Like the boss, and if you don't like the boss, make yourself like the boss.

If compatibility is "fair" in the cognitive area, you do not see eye to eye with your boss. You may disagree on the methods the boss uses, or you may feel invalidated. Possibly, you are taking it too personally when the boss corrects you or doesn't use your ideas. Or it may be that the boss is arrogant, egotistical, and always has to be "right" and win. If you see this for what it is (the boss's lack of confidence, lack of esteem, and insecurities), you may be more empathetic and tactful. Perhaps you are not managing your manager as well as you could. Then again, your boss could just not think like you, in which case it might behoove you to listen closely to what the boss says so you can understand the boss's mentality. Once you can acknowledge the boss's mentality, you have a better chance of introducing things in terms that your boss can understand. The secret to improving this mentality compatibility is to acknowledge, listen, and give good feedback so the boss knows you have heard. Try to get on the same page as the boss and understand his or her position, even if you don't agree with it. The boss must feel an understanding with you before he or she can entertain a disagreement with you.

The secret to winning over both the cognitive mentality and the mammal mentality is admiration. Find something genuine that you can admire, and then admire it. Egos and mammals value admiration. Your boss will not be inclined to dislike or invalidate someone who admires him or her.

If your compatibility is "fair" in the PFL area, it is probably because you and your boss are not in agreement about the purpose of either your work or his or her work. Setting a time with the boss to come to an understanding about this might be helpful. It may be that either you or your boss doesn't have a direction or see the bigger picture. By asking the boss about the vision he or she has of both of your jobs, you may be the catalyst to the realization of what the bigger picture is. Then, even if you aren't on the same page, maybe you can at least be in the same book.

If your compatibility is "poor" in any of the areas, it may take a lot of work to get there. You may want to think about whether you are being paid enough to make the effort or if you like your job enough to make the effort. One way to overcome an incompatibility with one mentality is to enhance the other ways you may be more compatible. For example, even if you think so differently from your boss that you can't bridge the gap, perhaps you can like him or her as a person. If you also have the same purpose, enhance that as well. Agreeing to disagree respectfully and with dignity may go far. Say things like, "I respect you and I know we are working toward the same goal, but I think we should take a different approach. Hey, I am who I am [smile]."

If you score below a "poor" in all of the areas, it is time to get a new boss. Transfer, or start looking for another job. It may be that your boss's ethics are incompatible with your own and you won't like yourself if you continue. It may be that your purposes are so different that you cannot continue.

4

NASTY CORPORATIONS, NASTY BOSSES, AND OTHER TAKERS

Corporations are likely to be the nastiest bosses. That's right—corporations. A corporation is a legal entity, like a person. However, a real person usually has motives higher than the profit motive—like family harmony, ethics, and doing what is *right*. A corporation may have the profit motive as the highest motive and may draw the line at doing what is *legal*. We know that things that are legal aren't always right (pornography, tying things up in court, over-charging, etc.).

Corporations pose the biggest problem in that executives are bound by a fixed set of corporate "rules." That is a backward mentality! The prefrontal lobe (a real person) should be at the helm, not a robotic set of rules. The rules come *after* a strategy is formed, and only human beings can have a strategy. With a corporation, you have the rules dictating to people who have a prefrontal lobe. That's a lesser mentality dictating to a greater mentality. Then there are the employees who work for the bosses who are bound by the lower mentality. These employees may have to go against their ethics on a daily basis so they can provide for their children, thereby prostituting themselves.

A corporate *environment* can create nasty bosses. People say that Hitler caused Germany to behave the way it did. Others say that Germany created Hitler.

Nasty Corporate Bosses May Be Takers

Takers may take your time, self-esteem, integrity, or other things that they are not entitled to. They victimize you with deception, invalidation, or unfairness. Remember the kids who would never let you play with their toys but would take yours? Those kids had a lot of excuses like: "I saw it first," "I was going to play with that," or just "Mine. Mine. Mine" (a direct quote from the seagulls in *Finding Nemo*). Those kids grew up physically, but some didn't grow up mentally. They attribute their stash to their own doing and still make excuses not to share. If you were like most kids, you stopped playing with them—a good move then, and a good move now if one of those kids ended up running your company. If takers need you, you may get some fairness here and there when they give you (resentfully) what you deserve, but as long as you work for this corporation, you will have to deal with that mentality.

Who are these takers? These are the bosses who abuse their authority. To some bosses, it's not about being fair or objective. It's not even about getting "enough." Even when they get wealthy, they don't take their couple million dollars into a corner of the world and enjoy life. Why? Because it's all about the game. It's all about dominance. There is really nothing wrong with dominance if you are talking about dominating a market. Even dominating people is OK, if you are fair about it and they agree to accept you as their alpha leader. The nasty corporations are the ones who dominate unfairly, deceptively, irresponsibly, against your will, and so on.

Nasty Corporate Bosses May Be Misers

Misering makes you feel as if you are "worth less." If you are being paid within the normal salary range, you do not feel as if you are being misered. If you are beneath the salary scale for your job, you feel misered. Children whose families cannot afford designer clothes will not feel misered, whereas children who know the family can afford it will feel misered if they are not given designer clothes like the other kids in their circle have. It's a form of abuse relative to the situation. The abuse part happens when you feel as if the person in authority is trying to tell you that you aren't good enough or you don't matter. The child gets the message, "You are not worth it." Of course, it is usually not about the child but the parent. It may help to know that when you are misered on the job by a profitable company, it is about the company and the miserly boss(es), not about you. Try not to take it personally as you look for a better opportunity.

Stop the Abuse

What happens to people who are abused on a regular basis? Sooner or later they reach a limit, but there's no telling what that limit may be. Usually victims become either apathetic or hostile. That's what happens. Read the newspapers. You are going to find it filled with the apathetic or hostile things people do. Look around. We are bursting at the seams with hostility—road rage, violence in the workplace, violence in the schools, and abuse at home. Or we apathetically turn to our addictions (alcohol, drugs, sex, work, etc.). How many of us anesthetize ourselves with food, for instance?

In so many cases of abuse, the abuser stops the abuse when the victim strikes back. Abusive fathers stop beating up their sons after the sons retaliate by beating up the fathers. Abuse is all about bullying and being able to get away with bullying or pushing someone around who is deemed weaker (or in the workplace deemed a subordinate). I choose to call it bullying because it is immature. The bullying is contagious. The president bullies the vice president who bullies the director who bullies the middle manager who bullies the manager who bullies the employee who bullies the spouse who bullies the kid who kicks the dog who chases the cat who tortures the mouse. You can bully (abuse) someone verbally or physically and even sexually. You can bully people by making up unfair rules; taking money from them (legally or illegally); holding their job over their head; making them jump through unnecessary hoops to get a mortgage; writing a lease in lawyer language that is all to your advantage; charging them thirty dollars for bouncing a check without even paying the check; charging horrendous late fees; charging exorbitant interest; charging high gas prices on the turnpike; and overcharging them for food at airports, sporting events, and other captive places. The abuse/bullying/victimizing is all about power and/or money. Some nasty bosses love the power trips knowing they can hurt you if they want to, using any and all nasty tactics just to feel better or more powerful than you.

In actuality, though, nasty individual bosses don't pose the biggest problem in today's society. In fact, we can learn what tactics they use and why they use them (power/dominance/the game), but that is only half the solution. The problem that is bigger than nasty bosses is our inability to identify corporate takers. The way the business world is set up today, we don't know who these takers are personally or even by face or name. Gone are the days of the mom-and-pop stores, where we could walk in and speak to the owners directly about any problems we had with their services.

Takers are not a new breed, but the old takers of a generation ago were, at least, visible. So, we had someone to hate, detest, and blame. At least they gave us *that* opportunity. The new takers are incognito. You never know who made up the process to victimize you. Was it the vice president of the company? The head of marketing? The local manager trying to make his profit deadlines so he could keep his job? Was it the employee who took it upon herself to blow you off so she could take a long lunch? And the power of knowing who were the takers was that we could actually *do* something about it—make them accountable, make sure there was justice, make sure no one else would be victimized in the future.

Today, the takers are the people behind the scenes—the unknown "untouchables." (But it's probably that kid that used to take your lunch money in school.) We don't know their names, and we don't get to complain to them.

The untouchables have people working for them—the "unjustables." And believe it or not, the unjustables are just as nasty as the untouchables. They take authority but claim no responsibility for it. The unjustables are the ones who may say, "*Just* doing my job." Some of the unjustables are merely concrete thinkers who function purely by the rules. They can't adjust to unique situations. They can't think out of the box. Others are people who lack substance and integrity but who are good soldiers carrying out the rules, however unjustly. They *just* want to make their stats and they will be happy. They don't see (or don't care to see) the big picture of how what they do affects others.

Today's takers can be the executives of corporations, managed care executives, mortgage underwriters, the owners of businesses like the hot dog vendors at the sporting events who charge you six dollars for a hot dog, or anyone who makes you feel victimized and misered and powerless because you can't fight back because you can't find the real takers. They're hiding behind their lackeys like cowards. You can't get angry at the bloke who sells you the hot dog. He is probably making minimum wage, and he is only the "prostitute" for the "pimp" hot dog boss, whom you never see.

If we are not careful, our society may become a pimp-prostitute society where we poor prostitutes carry out the bidding of our pimp bosses who lurk in the ivory towers counting the money and screaming for more so they can meet their greedy objectives. It is a systemic problem. Most of us are not severely victimized in one sitting, but we are victimized a little each day. It all adds up.

Although these misers and takers make us feel like victims and make us feel worthless, nobody really can *make* us feel a way unless we allow it. So get ready to arm yourself with defense tactics and learn what you can do about these nasty people.

What do we—the nontakers—do? We are limited by ethics and trying to do the right thing. How can we avoid being bullied any further? How do we avoid becoming apathetic or hostile, and how can we defend ourselves with dignity? Basically, how do we deal with the nasty bosses without stooping to their level? First, we need perspective.

One thing you can do initially is to (informally) consult with a trusted friend or coworker. Someone's objectivity is especially warranted if you are upset. Then, sleep on it and look at the issue the next morning. If it's an issue that needs to be addressed, try the following:

1. **Find the *what*.** When you are told, "It's company policy," ask to see it in writing. It may feel as if you are being obnoxious, but be persistent and don't stop until you get an answer. If it *is* policy, ask questions like, "How is that fair?" Make polite noise until someone understands. The executives may be so far removed from the workaday reality that they may need a "reality adjustment." You have a choice of feeling bullied and miserable or feeling assertive. If you hear a "just," as in "Just doing my job. I don't make the rules," then it's time for them to take some responsibility. Let them know you just want what is right. If you are not treated fairly, go to 2.

2. **Find the *who*.** Find the who that can answer your questions. Find the who that has the power to do something about the issue. There are a lot of Whos in Whoville, and one of those Whos has enough power and enough prefrontal lobe capacity to see the problem and correct it. If enough prostitutes complain and it starts taking away their productivity, their work becomes unprofitable. If enough prostitutes make an issue, the pimps will want to intervene and appease the prostitutes to make sure work gets done. If you wish to escalate, ask for the chairman of the board's address.

3. **Find out who proposed a certain policy and who seconded it.** In the movie *Christmas Vacation*, the executive who realized he had made an error in policy said, "Sometimes things look good on paper, when it doesn't actually work out well for people." Sometimes it's a matter of oversight for people on the board, and if you can call attention to the problem it may be eliminated.

4. **Be direct, and always speak your mind respectfully.** Confronting issues that bother you can show good results. Make sure you do your homework. Define the problem in specific terms and be ready to offer a solution if asked. While I was in Amsterdam I saw that happen on a regular basis. In Amsterdam, when the president of the company attends the company Christmas party, he may be asked, "Hey, why were our bonuses less than last year when the company made more profit this year?" Can you imagine an American doing that? We generally wimp out. If our questioning is done respectfully, politely, and in a friendly manner, it can show we are paying attention to the bigger picture. We are afraid some big authority figure is going to come down and smack our hands with a ruler or we will lose favor with the boss. Most bosses I know can handle it.

5. **If you are consistently treated with disrespect or invalidated, you may need to address two issues.** Suppose you are a secretary and your boss throws something on your desk and says, "Here. Type this . . . NOW!" Go ahead and type it. After typing it, get your boss alone, and let your boss know, "I typed this because you are my boss and I am your subordinate. In that way we are not equal. But we are

equal with regard to the respect and dignity that one human being owes to another. So as an equal in that way, I am asking you not to speak to me disrespectfully again." You need to discern the two separate messages and address them both. Chances are that your boss (who may not have respected you as much before) will respect you now.

6. **If you are misered, first assess your opportunities in other companies, the profitability of your company, and your value to the boss.** If all are positive, ask the boss for fifteen minutes to discuss something important to you. Present your salary findings. You may want to ask the boss if he or she views you as valuable to the company. If the boss says, "I will look into it," or some such vague thing you have heard in the past to put you off, ask if he or she can put you on the calendar for next week. If you finally get a raise and your boss is a miser, prepare yourself to do the same next year. You may want to show the miser boss how giving you a raise is going to be a good thing financially for both you and the company as, for example, your productivity will increase as your experience increases.

7. **If your boss is a bully, don't be an easy target.** Make it painful for your boss to invalidate or disrespect you. The most painful areas to kick the boss are usually in the ego or profit. You could be passive-aggressive and just get "sick" and have to go home after an invalidation (and there goes your productivity for the day). It may not take the boss long to figure out that her or his behavior is making you sick. But a better way is to not kick the boss but

paint the bigger picture by exposing her or him and say something like, "Hey, you're embarrassing me in front of everyone." You could say, "What did you just say to me? Say it again. I didn't get the full essence." When my brother was in sixth grade, there was a bully that picked on him during recess. We tried everything (being nice, trying to be friends, etc.), but nothing worked. Finally, I said, "You are going to have to hurt him." My brother said, "What!? He'll beat me up!" I told him he was going to get beat up anyway. The next day my brother ran up and kicked the bully in the shinbone as hard as he could. My brother got beat up, but the bully never bothered him again. (P.S.: Don't take this literally. Find a figurative way to kick the corporate bully in the shins.) (P.P.S.: I realize this one recommendation may be stooping to their level. Use it as a last resort.)

It's a hassle to do these things. It's sometimes embarrassing. But it's better than kicking the dog, and your shoe would be aimed in a more accurate direction.

Legal Issues

You can't be fired for asking to see company policy, or for finding out who made up the rule, or for being respectfully direct, or for notifying the boss of the limits and boundaries of your relationship, or for asking for a raise, or for exposing your boss's personal tactics. Once I had a boss that I knew didn't like me. I didn't like him, either. He was always chewing me out in front of others. Finally, during one of his outbursts, I said, "I know you don't like me, and I don't like you either, but I am going to do a good job for you anyway. Now, could you do your part to stop embarrassing me in front of everyone?" All I did was say it like it was. When you say it like it is, you can move on from there. I stopped pussyfooting. He stopped finding excuses to yell at me. Both of us ended up liking not-liking each other. I think he actually overcompensated by doing more for me than others to prove he was objective (heh heh).

For *big* issues, there are laws to protect whistle-blowers. You really can't be fired for going to the newspapers on an issue, although this would usually be a last resort. If it is a big enough issue that affects others, the newspapers may take it on. Otherwise they may tell you to go through normal channels within your company. The bottom line is, if you do your job and you express valid issues, there is probably less of a chance that you will be fired than if you are seen and not heard. Your approach should be to give your immediate boss a chance to rectify the situation. Even if you know your boss won't or can't rectify the situation, it is common courtesy to inform. Once I went right to an executive for a problem I had because I knew he was the only one that could fix it. He told me that he was going to pretend we never talked and that I should see my direct manager. It was good advice. It was better to let my management know what was going on.

When you point out problems that may have detrimental legal consequences for the company, that may be motivation to resolve them quickly. Most companies do not like personnel problems and are motivated to resolve them because they are time-consuming, and time is money.

Some takers may be concerned about other issues of legality, but only to the point of how much more they can get before things change. If a law changes that protects people from being victimized, the takers start looking for another way to capitalize on their greed, and they will find another way. They may increase their big salaries from the corporation, running it into the ground, and then look for other corporations they can hide in.

This type of mentality always amazes me. When I was consulting at a jail, some of the more brilliant inmates there were capable of earning a very good living by running legitimate businesses. Yet, they preferred to victimize people. Why? It's about *domination*. There's that word again. Some dogs just want other dogs to show their necks. Other dogs take it one step further and urinate on the other dogs. The ones in jail have been caught doing it illegally. Other criminal minds do it legally—because they *can*. They enjoy the thrill of screwing society and getting away with it. These people have to do it up close and personal. They are not the same as the ones who hide in the backroom.

Just because something is legal doesn't mean it's not done with criminal intent. Some of our laws are old and outdated and do not apply to the new technologies. These are some indications of the criminal mind:

- Deceitfulness or conning others for profit or pleasure. Deception runs rampant in so many of our

businesses. The agreements are so long and there is
so much fine print written in legalese.

- Reckless disregard for the safety of others. This is
  where the financial analysts estimate the defects of a
  product and weigh out the cost of lawsuits versus the
  cost of recalling the product.
- Failure to honor financial obligations. This is where a
  company may deliberately set itself up to file low-
  level bankruptcy to "give their suppliers a haircut"
  (pay less than what they owe).
- Lack of remorse. This is where company executives
  show no conscience or the conscience takes second
  place to other goals.
- Repeated lying.
- Rationalizing mistreatment or hurt to another. This
  tactic blames the victim for not being aware of the
  negative situation he or she faces.

All these can be carried out legally. Can you fire someone
just before they retire? Yes. Can you raise the telephone
rates to forty cents a minute when the going rate is five
cents? Yes. Is it legal to write up a long telephone contract
with the forty cents a minute in small print? Yes. Is it legal
to take ten dollars out of someone's wallet? No, you may
go to jail for that. But it is the same mentality. Some of our
legal entities reach into our pockets for a lot more than ten
dollars. Deceitfulness is *in*. It's no wonder that we have
more people in jail, per capita, than ever. Many of the peo-

ple in jail do the same things our legal authorities do. If they could just learn the legal ways to do those things, they wouldn't have to go to jail.

The Squeeze

The systemic problem we have in our society comes out as a feeling in the individual that I call "the squeeze." Most people know exactly what I am talking about. All they have to do is search their feelings and they experience the squeeze. The squeeze is a part of us now. It exists in daily life as a low-level angst in most of us. We have been studied and analyzed to the point where "they" know how to squeeze the most productivity out of us. There have been so many studies on productivity and life span that we have become fairly predictable. We can be assessed fairly accurately as to how long we are going to live, what our most productive years are going to be, and when our health problems will start. Did you know that most people die within two years of retirement? Isn't that interesting?

Look at all the downsizing we have done: a popular action. Even when it isn't necessary, some management just thinks it's "in" to downsize. Some companies are run by skeleton crews. And it's not just companies—it's our nonprofit organizations too, like our schools. Our teachers are worked to the bone. Many don't have time to be a tremendous influence to a kid (as they may have idealistically fantasized about in college). There is a study plan that has to be done, and the children are made to be competitive with other schools so the higher-ups can be acknowledged for doing such a great job. Our teachers don't have time to spend with that one more kid with an attention deficit— that one more kid that they could have made a difference with . . . if they only had time. We are losing track of the bigger picture.

Very few of us have any extra time now. Even when we are driving from one place to another, we don't have time to contemplate because our cell phone is ringing or we have to call someone. We have taken productivity to an unnatural state.

There are plenty of casualties too. If you get sick or have a nervous breakdown, you can't depend on your job to be there for you. If you have a good lawyer, maybe you will get disability. If not, you just have to wait until you get better and hope your house and car don't get repossessed. If you reach a point that you can't pay your lawyer, your lawyer will abandon you.

The old values are disappearing from the corporations and organizations that employ people. Corporations are not as dedicated to their employees as they once were. There is not as much respect for the individual—not as much empathy, commitment, work ethics (fairness), fortitude, integrity, or conviction.

Conviction. Now there is an interesting word. I don't mean conviction like a prison sentence. I mean the second definition of conviction involving the human spirit: "Convinced with strong belief. Justice." You still find conviction here and there, but the corporations and organizations are finding it more and more costly (i.e., less and less cost-effective). Let's face it: it seems costly to be fair and just— to avoid "squeezing" your employees. But in the long run, corporations are finding out it is actually more costly. People want to be paid more if there is less job security and the cost of training new employees adds up.

What Are We Willing to Put Up With?

Are you getting ticked off yet? I don't mean to tick you off, but I do want you to get in touch with that feeling about it. You know . . . the feeling of being "squeezed." And I want to expose a lot of tactics of the takers, and that will probably tick them off.

The definition of evil as adapted from M. Scott Peck's *People of the Lie* says that evil can be an overt or covert act. Doing something to hurt someone is evil, and so is doing nothing so that people get hurt. In Connecticut, if you are a doctor or nurse and you drive by an accident without stopping, you are in big trouble. That's one of the main problems with nasty bosses and nasty corporations. It's what they *don't* do and what they *don't* plan that can cause so much grief. When they don't consider the human element and fairness to human beings, they are acting as criminals do. Psychopaths don't necessarily set out to hurt people. It's just that they are not concerned if they do and don't factor that in. So many times you will hear criminals say things like, "I didn't mean to shoot him. He was just in the line of fire when I was robbing the bank." They don't seem to understand that if they weren't robbing the bank, the shooting wouldn't have happened!

Wouldn't you like to kick ass and name names? But no one wants to listen to it. No one wants to be reminded of the junk they go through every day. Especially when we know it's a systemic problem and we feel useless about being able to do something about it. But doesn't *somebody* have to do *something* about it *sometime*? Aren't "they" going to do something about all this? "They" is you, baby. There is no other "they."

We (which includes you) are very upset about the greed and lack of ethics going on in our society. We are upset about the excessive executive pay. We are upset about the mutual fund scandals with managers making money for their own personal selves from our retirement accounts. We loathe the corporate scandals. What do we do? We might watch another Arnold movie where the bad guy gets his just dues. We might flip a finger and yell at someone who is driving aggressively. Then maybe we feel better for a while.

As U.S. citizens, we are part of the worst and the best. A major part of the world wants to be like us. Some people risk their lives to come to this country. We are the most influential country in the world today, and we get respect. Some of us violate that respect in the worst way. We abhor greed and we are happy when some greedy snake gets caught by the legal system. People who make small wages resent companies that pay executives to excess. Yet we are also forgiving and generous. If some wrongdoer sits down with Barbara Walters and fesses up with remorse on national television, we forgive ("Miss Manners Regrets," *BusinessWeek*, January 12, 2004).

What we do about all this boils down to our own personal ethics and values. The number one thing that is going to matter the most is what we decide we are going to put up with. Let me demonstrate:

First example: we do not put up with a parent beating a child these days. That is something that has changed from forty years ago. Today, if you smack your child around in the supermarket, you are liable to make the 5:00 P.M. news. What overcame this problem? Knowledge of its effects on adult children, knowledge of better methods of discipline, and conscience. We *can* change things.

Second example: forty years ago, civil rights were not enforced. Things have changed. People don't put up with that. What overcame that disrespect? Pride, integrity, suffering in the short run for respect in the long run.

Third example: forty years ago, an alcoholic was considered to be someone who was weak-willed and didn't give a damn. Now we don't put up with that definition. Alcoholism is considered an illness, and a lot more people are recovering. What overcame this ignorance? Education.

So what do we have so far?

- Knowledge
- Conscience
- Pride
- Integrity
- Suffering
- Education

If we are truly tired of being bullied and invalidated by a boss—if we are truly tired of being overlooked, not accounted for, treated unfairly, and having our feelings ignored by a corporate entity—we might have to give knowledge to those in power. We might have to suffer the consequences of being confrontational. If "they" are not the way we want "them" to be, then we have to make it hard for "them" to be that way. Every time our conscience makes us fuss about something that is not fair, we make it a better world for our children. Every time we enable someone or some company, we make it worse for our children and ourselves. The woman who enables her alcoholic husband by calling in sick for him or taking a beating when he is drunk is committing an act of omission that propagates and guarantees the future of his alcoholism. She guarantees dysfunction for herself, himself, and their children. She is no saint. She is the devil's helper.

Are you going to be the devil's helper? Are your children going to have to put up with the same invalidation and unfairness that you do? I bet it was difficult for the first people who advocated on behalf of a child who was being abused. I am sure they were looked at as "interfering" in the parents' discipline and dominating the "rights" of the parents to discipline. I bet the first black people to refuse to put up with disrespect had a rough time. The first alcoholics to attend meetings were thought to be hopeless, and their families thought their efforts were futile.

It really is unfair that you should have to confront people who should know better. I should know. I wrote a book called *Nasty People*. I thought it was unfair for me to have to confront people who should know better than to invalidate me. For years I didn't confront them, and during those years, I had the makings of ulcers three times, and I drank a lot. I blamed the ulcers on spicy food. I didn't blame the drinking on anyone. I wasn't an alcoholic . . . I jussht liked to drink . . . thash all! Right! Denial is a wonderful thing until you cough up blood and start thinking about having a drink *before* work.

So what's it going to be, my friend? Ulcers, drinking, overeating, shame, poor self-esteem, the squeeze, anxiety? Or confronting; being labeled as "too sensitive"; making a fuss; suffering; having integrity, courage, pride, and confidence; educating; and making a better world for your children?

If you choose to confront, you may have to learn some skills. When I first started standing up for myself in the throes of being invalidated, I wasn't very good at it. The first couple times, I was very immature, like a baby learning how to walk. I actually called a guy names in the midst of a professional meeting. Hey, I am pretty good at it now, though. With a lot of practice, I was eventually able to use a sense of humor or direct confrontation to expose the invalidation. I turned lemons into lemonade and sold one million copies of *Nasty People*. Make it hard for someone to bully you. Make it not fun for them, not productive for them, not profitable for them. Keep this strategy in the back of your mind.

Some people are rational-cognitive people, and some people are cause-effect people. Bullies are usually cause-effect people like the one my brother kicked in the shins at recess. If cause-effect bullies don't see, feel, or get affected by the consequences of their actions . . . there were no consequences. If a bully (corporation or boss) is deceitful, lies, has no remorse, and doesn't respond to the greater good, it's time for consequences. Legal ones. Ones we can but don't use.

- Writing the chair of the board (registered mail, return receipt)
- Asking to see someone who can make a fair decision
- Being a pain in the butt—making unfairness unprofitable

We may have to face dragons. But nowadays, dragons don't look like dragons. They are incognito but are easily unmasked once they are identified as takers. Not all bank executives, managed care executives, or hot dog vendor bosses are takers—only the ones who step over the line of ethics. Only those who do not differentiate between profit and greed, and right or wrong.

One of the ways to stop gossip is to search for the people who started the rumor. You may never find them, but they know you are looking and they stop gossiping about you. They don't like to be confronted. That's why they try to ruin you behind your back. It's the same with some bullies. If you start heading for them, it scares the heck out of them. They really don't want to own up to what they do. These are the passive-aggressive criminal minds.

So what do you do?

- Find out who they are.
- Confront them personally (respectfully and legally, face to face, or by letter).
- Expose them. (State the consequences their actions had on you. Tell others.)

I have been thinking about the problems in the corporate system for a few decades, and it has been of great interest to me. I have always endeavored to see the big picture of things. Can one person change the systemic process? Not alone. In unity there is strength, my friend. Didn't someone say that once? Oh, yes, I believe his name was Lincoln. We enable the bullies by being lackadaisical. We don't participate. Most of us don't vote. We are too busy to deal with things or we don't know how or we don't think we can, so these situations persist. Rectifying this situation is about *ethics*. We don't let people attack our country. We just don't put up with it. It is a strong patriotic ethic that we are willing to die for. Yet we are willing to be held hostage by a nasty boss because we don't want to risk the embarrassment of invalidation. We are willing to be ripped off by a corporation because we are too embarrassed to make a scene. Our ethics need to change with regard to this stuff. Confront your boss (human to human). Make a scene (it won't kill you). If you do it legally, the police won't take you away. If you do it within your rights, you won't get into trouble.

Let's think out of the box.

Outside-the-Box Solutions

A long, long time ago, there were objections to the forming of corporations. Back when the legislation was being drawn, some people felt that corporations would be a means for certain persons to evade responsibility. And they were right. President Lincoln warned us about the power of corporations. In 1832 the state of Pennsylvania revoked the charter of ten banks that were operating contrary to the public interest. Nevertheless, corporations were allowed to form. They were supposed to operate as individuals and were declared a "natural person" in 1886. That was the only way they were allowed to exist—by operating as an *individual*.

The "Mental Health" of Corporations

As a psychologist, and as someone who was in management for a large corporation for years, and as someone who participated in consulting for other organizations, I can tell you this: if corporations are supposed to be persons, many corporations have mental health problems. If I had to diagnose some of them as legal persons, I would have to diagnose many with dissociative identity disorder (multiple personality disorder) and antisocial personality disorder (psychopathic personality disorder). Many times the right hand doesn't know what the left hand is doing. And there is no conscience, other than the conscience that each employee is *allowed* to have. A real person usually has a conscience and usually knows what promises they made yesterday. A person who has a multiple personality disorder is "Joe" one day and "Harry" the next day, and Joe may not know what Harry did the day before. When someone contacts me, they get a person with a conscience to do the right thing, not someone with a preconceived set of rules that may or may not be fair.

They are going to get Jay today and Jay tomorrow, and, barring Alzheimer's, they will get *consistency*. When people talk to me, they talk to the decision maker. When you talk to a corporation, you usually get someone who can say no, but that person is not authorized to say yes. If you call my home, you won't get a recorder that says, "I am currently busy talking with other corporations. Please stay on the line. I value your call. It will be approximately (beep) twenty minutes to answer your call. Please don't hang up, as you will lose your turn in the queue." (Music plays.) Do you think a corporation is going to spend twenty minutes waiting for me on hold so that I can save the overhead by not hiring enough people to answer the phone? Heck no!

One of the ways to approach the whole problem of no ethics, lack of conviction, or multiple personality is to have the corporation declared incompetent by a mental health professional. I told you we were going to think out of the box. But a "natural person" is subject to this.

The corporation is an individual, right? What do we do with people who are destructive to themselves or others? Well, we get a psychiatrist or psychologist to have them committed to the state hospital. I wonder who would go? Would it be the president or the board chair? A couple days in the loony bin might just be what they need. Shoot 'em with a little Haldol or Thorazine in the ass and I bet their "type A" personalities would calm down and they would become more rational.

I am just kidding around (about the Thorazine, not the declaration of incompetence—they have to be fit to deal with real people). I realize that most corporate CEOs and presidents are ethical and have the best interest of everyone in mind, and they are under pressure to make sure the company is solvent. If they don't make a profit, then many people may be out of work. But once you start going over the line and trading ethics and justice for profit, you can't go down with the ship with any integrity. Some executives would throw the women and children overboard to keep the boat afloat for themselves. They should be shot in the ass with more than Thorazine.

Customer and Employee Satisfaction

If you are looking for a good company to work for, where can you go to check the business ethics of a corporation? There are surveys for the larger corporations, but . . . ah, well . . . we need something like that, don't we? The Internet auction site eBay has a good system. You can check exactly what percentage of customers have been satisfied. Likewise, we need a system that can give feedback on employee satisfaction. Would you pay a small fee to access an Internet company that measured customer satisfaction and employee satisfaction? I would. Some bright people and some bright lawyers are going to read this book and see a purpose for themselves in this. Many organizations would welcome it. It would get other organizations back to their purpose—to serve. This would put the power back into the people's hands. *We* would decide who is improper and who is worthy of our business skills. With the Internet, we could tally the number of satisfied customers and dissatisfied customers. We could decide who is fair and unfair. Who is organized and who is a multiple personality. Which corporation is humane and which one is a jerk. This would work well for customers, also.

Without conviction, there is no one monitoring. Most banks make a huge profit when you bounce a check. It costs them very little. Past bank presidents have appeared on television and stated publicly how unfair it is to charge so much for a bounced check. I thought the government was the only organization allowed to punish people for wrongdoings. There is nothing wrong with making a huge profit on something. This is America. If a good marketing manager advertises a better mousetrap and sells it for half the price of regular mousetraps and it costs her or him very little to make it so he or she makes millions, I applaud that, and I will buy that mousetrap. A "taker" is a bad marketing manager who takes advantage of a situation and holds a person hostage in a captive situation to pay. That is no different from bullying people for their lunch money. You see, these bullies grow up and become bank executives, in charge of collecting bounced-check fees. Actually, the executives are probably following the rules dictated by the organization, whether or not they think it's right.

Unfortunately, we are a "bunch of individuals" in this country. We do not unite as much as we should. Not enough of us have written to our politicians. We don't have time to do so because 80 percent of us are busy working for corporations.

We don't normally think about pressing criminal charges against corporations. Yet, they *are* "natural persons" under the law. There is a criminal charge called "theft by deception" that many of them can be charged with. Try it, sometime, if you think you have been victimized that way. Someone is supposed to go to jail.

Conscience

When people started incorporating, we left out something very important. We forgot to incorporate a conscience. Again, nasty bosses model this example. There are so many lawsuits that are taking up space, time, and money (*yours*) because a corporation wants to tie certain things up in court to buy time or to get the plaintiff to barter. Isn't that wrong? If a corporation is "unconscionable" and therefore a danger to others, shouldn't it be "decorporated"?

Truly, if a corporation is unable to act as a person, it should not be one. Most people don't care if a corporation has a sexual identity, but they do care if the corporation has a conscience. This possibility of decorporation may motivate companies to communicate with customers in a more uniform way. It may motivate companies to follow a code of ethics even if it cuts into their profits.

Before "decorporation," a company might be provided with the opportunity to fix itself so that it could operate as an individual. First, there should be a diagnosis by a competent professional—possibly an industrial psychologist who has experience and knowledge in the proper areas of psychology and business. This person, too, should confer with other "corporate therapists" to identify the strategies needed for the corporation to function as a legal person entity. The strategies should then be turned over to the corporation to analyze the means by which they can accomplish their objectives. A deadline is necessary throughout the process. If two corporations have intercourse outside of merger, perhaps a spiritual adviser could be brought in. (Just kidding about that last one.)

Accountability

In addition to lack of conscience, our organization authorities are lacking accountability, as someone of flesh and blood might have to another.

A generation ago, we had the mom-and-pop businesses. If you thought Pop ripped you off, you could go down to his business location and get in his face. If it was an oversight, Pop or Mom would make good on it, and the situation would be resolved. If Pop didn't make good on it, you could tell all your friends and relatives how he ripped you off, and he would lose business. The corporations put Mom and Pop out of business because they could offer us products cheaper. The corporations used to be nice to their customers and tried to be fair by giving the power to be just to the people entrusted to work for them. Things have changed. The corporations are now into downsizing or merging, and the executives have taken the power to say yes away from the entrusted employees so that they don't "give away the store" and do any of those fair things that result in the profit line being lowered.

Good Boss, Nasty Corporation

These days, bosses have a lot more pressure to produce yet have a lot less power to do it with. In the old days, people expected to work for a company for life, so it was important to them to make sure the company survived, and it was important to maintain working relationships. Now, people know they may not be working for a company in two years, and they have to have their own retirement account. They are not tied to the company, and they could care less if it folds. The company is not going to bail them out if they get sick or incapacitated, so they need to make as much as they can. We usually model our authority figures. Twenty years ago, there was more mentoring and nurturing in our careers. Now some bosses feel they have to wear two faces to survive. It turns them into "Benedict Arnold" bosses— bred by the needs or wants of the corporation and following the rules. It fosters a covert form of ruthlessness. Many of our authority figures have become almost forced to be more like "takers," so we tend to model that behavior too. We prostitutes (again, not sexually speaking) want more money if there is no retirement fund or good hospitalization plan. Companies that had formerly good ethical management may introduce policies that are unfair and unethical, and if management doesn't carry out those policies, they get axed (e.g., laying off senior people to hire new, inexperienced people for less money).

Working with a corporation that cares less for the individual and has less fairness (bowing to profit motive), the bosses today have less to work with. It is tempting to use the lower forms of management techniques such as intimidation, fear, and threats instead of motivation, respect, and validation. Ethical standards in business have dropped considerably, and it's hard to be ethical in an unethical world.

So let's take a look at the psyche of our "natural person"—the corporation. I am going to have to call it an "it" because it is neither male nor female. Its prime directive is profit. Secondarily, it has a directive to obey the laws. The only ethics and fairness it is bound by come from the laws—not the normal ethics and humanity of a real person. Reputation is important to it because a dip in reputation means less profit, and profit is absolutely necessary for survival. It also has a team of lawyers that can slap down or delay any lawsuits. Some corporations have a set of company beliefs, but these can change at any time via stockholders via the board of directors.

I don't believe that the drafters of corporations set out to take advantage of people. Just like human beings, an organization seems to operate on Maslowe's hierarchy of needs, which says that if food, clothing, and shelter are not met, a real human might not be above doing some unconscionable things to satisfy those needs. Likewise, if an organization is trying to survive, the only way is through making a profit, and it may do some unconscionable things to stay afloat. An organization really is a lesser natural person than a real human, and as such, organizations make poor masters. Organizations are meant to serve, not to enslave. They are meant to serve the public and the people who make up the organization. Any good businessperson knows that a business thrives by providing a good product or service. Good bosses know that they are there to support the people that work for them. The element of self-serving deteriorates the entire setup. A self-serving employee makes a self-serving boss who makes a self-serving executive who makes more self-serving bosses who make more self-serving employees. This deterioration truly makes us into a "bunch of individuals" trying to beat each other out and creating an environment where the taker mentality has domain.

What is the solution? It starts with you and me. We have to have enough personal integrity to do what is right despite the suffering we may endure. We have to have enough courage to *not* enable the takers. We have to create the ethic that it's not cool to victimize people or be greedy. We can do it. We have already shown we can. It's not cool to beat your kids. It's not cool to disrespect fellow Americans. It *is* cool to be a recovering alcoholic. And those are only a few things we have changed with a change in ethics.

So, if you are tired of selling out and you have a nasty corporation bullying you, where are the shins you can kick on a corporation? They are located in the profit.

How do you deal with the flesh and bones type of nasty boss? Some traits seem to pervade:

- They are usually self-consumed and self-serving. They may not be motivated to understand others, or they may be incapable or so involved with their own tunnel vision that they can't. They may want to understand others for their own benefit—still self-consumed and self-serving.

- They usually care about what certain select people think (people who can take their power away).

Chapter 2 is full of ways to handle bosses in the flesh. Many of the same things apply to corporations. In either case, there are certain things that should never be negotiated:

- Integrity
- Ethics
- Personal responsibility
- Dignity

5

PROFESSIONAL ADVICE

Most of this chapter is derived from advice from people who are (or were) recent top-level executives, managers, and supervisors for small, medium, and large companies. Some of the interviewees were people who provide services for the whole organization directly under the auspices of executives. The interviews with these people were confidential, and you will find only a few of them listed in the Acknowledgments to protect privacy and ensure candidness. I am very fortunate to have personal access to such dynamic individuals. The environment is the big picture. Before I get advice, I like to know *why*. The "why" is the big picture, so we are going to spend a little time showing/exposing the big picture. The lack of a big picture can have disastrous results . . . such as the electricity being off for several days on the East Coast. When we operate like a "bunch of individuals," this kind of thing can happen. I would like you to be in the prefrontal lobe for this section—*seeing* the bigger picture.

Job Climate

All agree that the job climate has changed from twenty years ago. In order to talk about bosses, we have to recognize the environment that the bosses work in (the big picture). So let's use our prefrontal lobe to look at the patterns and themes of this day and age. If we can do that, we can form some of our own personal approaches. I will just replay/adapt the interviews.

The consensus is that there are more nasty bosses than ever. Business trends are creating environments that require bosses to be more "ruthless." The downsizing mania has prompted the emergence of a new type of boss. Many companies were cutting costs due to the downward economy some years back, and it is still going on. Companies cut costs significantly by getting rid of senior people and hiring new people at starting salaries. The managers who did not have the stomach for making these cuts got dumped along with the senior employees. Organizations were combining (through mergers and buyouts) and then identifying employees and management that were "duplicates" and phasing them out or laying them off. The ones that were left may have been given impossible workloads, and if they couldn't measure up, they would be let go down the road.

This simplemindedness produced the bottom lines: increasing profits and cutting costs. Many people were working out of fear and desperation, putting in sixty- or seventy-hour weeks trying to do the work of two or more people so they wouldn't get canned. Many of our organizations operated on skeleton crews with people who did not truly know the business. These buyouts are still going on, and all the related dynamics are still happening. However, it is more recognized that it is more profitable to maintain some expertise and keep the morale up so that pesky class-action lawsuits don't originate and dig into the profits.

Individuation

The process of negative individuation occurs when a person becomes "other" than the group. The bosses who carry out the hatcheting actions mostly have to individuate from the people (so much for teamwork and a common cause). It creates a conflict of interest because the boss is now the one to be reckoned with rather than a respected leader. A similar conflict of interest happens with managed health care companies. Their purpose is to provide health care (pay), and their counterpurpose is to make a profit by lowering costs (not pay). It is hard to have trust and faith in a conflicted relationship with a company. People individuate themselves, and it becomes "every man for himself, every woman for herself, and let me get what I can while I can." (The victim eventually mimics the perpetrator.) Teamwork becomes impossible when people are keeping secrets for job security and fearfully individuating. A positive individuation occurs when a family member is strong enough to go out on his or her own (e.g., a child leaves for college). In the work environment, it would be when an employee has learned enough to be promoted to another department for a better job.

Other-Country Labor

The labor market overseas does not help allay the fears people have of losing their jobs. It used to be that blue-collar workers had to worry about their jobs being moved out of the country. Now, white-collar workers are in the same position. When you call a help desk or customer service, you are likely to get someone in India.

It is just as Alvin Toffler said in his book *Future Shock*: we are getting culture shock. Things are changing so fast. We are getting culture shock . . . not only because of our own culture changing so fast, but the people on the other end of the phone don't respond to the same cues and don't have the same assumptions we have about life. I am not sure if these changes are for better or worse in the long run, but I am sure it psychologically places many of us in fear for our jobs and makes us work harder, longer, and with more angst.

Buyouts

In talking about buyouts, the executives who would know say the following: many times when there's a buyout, the company that was bought gets ravaged (sold assets, increased debt, downsized senior employees, etc.). There is a new breed of bosses—people who are not limited by conscience or fairness, but good soldiers who do what they have to do to accomplish the objectives set forth by the organization. The bottom line: profitability. Sometimes it is *necessary* to take this approach. Other times it is just greedy. Some companies were bought out every two years by a different profiteer, each time increasing debt, diminishing reputation, and leaving unemployed, exhausted, or fearful employees. "Business is war" is a motto leading to unethical but legal actions on the part of the "warmongers." Meanwhile, the businesses that suffered or were "killed" may have been businesses that came from the old school with mottos like, "A fair day's wage for a fair day's work" or "A fair exchange for a service or product." Business ethics were thrown out the window as long as it was "legal." Organizations claimed bankruptcy just to lower their debt (referred to as giving their suppliers a "haircut"). The mentality of bosses had to change in order for them to survive, and those noble bosses who couldn't change were replaced by more foreboding creatures who didn't have so many ethical quibbles.

One company consulted its lawyers about the way to lay off a large group of highly paid people. The result was this:

One day, this group of people was herded into the auditorium. There were security people and lawyers present. There was no explanation given other than they were not

needed anymore because their work had been transferred
to the buying company. They were given two minutes to
pack up their desks and hit the road. Very efficient. No non-
sense. And very nasty. Some of these people had been at
that company for fifteen, twenty, twenty-five years. It was
unethical and inhumane, but legal.

Authority Figures

We have lost faith and trust in our authority figures significantly over the past couple of decades thanks to govern-
mental and corporate scandals. With authority figures come
the considerations of fairness, integrity, objectivity, faith,
trust, respect, loyalty, dedication, higher purpose, ethics,
and so on. We are getting to the point where we can't associate these terms with our authority figures. There is no
sense of purpose or teamwork. Organizations have spent a
lot of money trying to foster teamwork. The money was
wasted. Teamwork cannot be fostered without a purpose,
and the purpose of profit doesn't really touch the human
soul. It just makes us do what we have to do to get by and
get our money. Americans are known for accomplishing our
purposes. We put a man on the moon, and most everyone
who worked on that project had a sense of purpose no matter how lowly their jobs were. The management mentality
of today does not want to deal with personnel problems
(praise and promotions, acknowledgment, sickness, family
problems, personality conflicts, etc.). The mentality is simple: you work; we pay you. That's like a famous basketball

star in a national commercial saying, "I am not a role model." Guess what? He *is* a role model. It doesn't matter if a boss signed up to be an authority figure or not. It doesn't matter if the boss wants it or not. That's like saying, "I want to jump in the pool, but I don't want to get wet."

Bullying

In one sense, Americans do not sit well with being victimized. One of our states has the motto "Live free or die." That motto is just one that exemplifies our navigation to higher purposes. We can get organized and patriotic when there is an external threat to our way of life. But we get kind of wimpy when we are bullied by our own. We accept bullying as a rite of passage in this country. Everyone has to go through it, right? European countries don't look at it that way, and it shows. When there is a meeting with a vice president of a company in Europe, people ask whatever is on their mind. We don't do that here. We don't want to tick off the VP. The ones who do speak up cause the other employees to whisper to each other, "I can't believe they said that!" People in Europe have more personal security (e.g., health care for all, good unemployment packages, etc.), but how did they get that? By fearing that the bully was going to take their lunch money? I think not.

There was a track supervisor for a railroad who replaced a retired supervisor. The rail yard had been neglected and was in need of repair. The new supervisor had been unfairly critical to nearly everyone who worked under him. One night, fifteen rail cars derailed in his domain. The cost in track repair and to rerail the cars was significant. High-ranking officials traveled long distances to observe the damage and analyze the cost. It was a substantial loss. The officials were so angry they began to chastise and berate the supervisor and even threaten him with dismissal in front of his employees for allowing the derailment to happen. The employees looked at it as a comeuppance for the way he treated people in the past. No one came to his defense.

The dragon gets slayed by his own sword.

Purpose

Perhaps we have run out of higher purposes for the moment. After all, we have already achieved wealth. We are one of the richest countries in the world. For the most part our material needs are met. We are used to advancement, but it looks like times have changed. The purpose with employers now is not the promotions and advancements of the past. Individuals in this country work more hours per year than people in almost all other countries in the world, per capita. We live to work. Those in other countries work to live. The people derive their purposes from things other than work.

Depression

There is a fear that we are going to have another depression. This one won't be like the one in 1929. This one will be due to the skeleton crews operating our businesses.

These businesses were set up by people who knew what they were doing and knew the business. That knowledge is diminishing greatly. I see it in computer science programs. The students are taught to program in several different languages, but most are never taught how a computer really works. These languages were created and set up by people who actually knew the computer. Most of them are gone (dead or retired), and now we have a lot of people who know the languages. What if we need a new language or the language has a bug in it? Heaven forbid.

There is a sweater company in Pennsylvania, and no one in the entire company knows how to knit a sweater. They just know how to operate the machinery. The management has been totally changed so that no one—not management or employees—knows much about the business. They are operating on autopilot. The next crash may happen from a "Stop in Tasking due to Unilateral Information Deficiency" (STUPID). Our businesses are becoming stupid. Are we just a bunch of individuals? Is anyone watching (i.e., seeing the big picture)? When we are kids, our parents watch out for us and they have the bigger picture in sight, we think. We like to think that someone is watching over us (FDA, government, police, etc.). When I was a kid, I lived on a farm and had a pet bull we called Spot. He was just like a dog, except that he grew up to be huge. He was protective of me. I'll never forget the feeling I had when the neighborhood bully tried to get me down and my thousand-pound bull knocked him across the barnyard. I felt safe, secure, and special. That feeling has left the work world for many of us. The fear of a depression was felt by a majority of the execs I interviewed, although some thought there would not be a general economic depression but a depression for certain pockets of people in our society who have been disenfranchised.

On the Positive Side

We have always been adaptable people. Whereas other countries and peoples are burdened by procedure and culture, we are frontier oriented. We have been through these types of changes before. Around the Civil War time, about 50 percent of Americans were farmers or tied to farming. Now, it is just a little over 2 percent, and we are not starving. We migrated to industry. Then steel mills started closing down and we sent those jobs overseas. We migrated to white-collar jobs (programmers, help desks, loan officers, etc.). Now those jobs are going overseas. Technology allows us to pick up the phone for computer help and get someone in the Philippines to answer our call. We are truly becoming a world economy. Maybe there will be no more starving people. Change is usually good for the mentality. We become less narcissistic. We realize that twenty dollars a month really does provide food and medical care for a kid in the Philippines. With that, we realize how truly fortunate we are. It expands our prefrontal lobe capability when we see the bigger picture. And the picture *is* getting bigger. We might become happier with our Honda Pilot SUV even if we did want the Acura more. We are a society in transition right now. The victimization and profiteering will stop soon because we will stop it. Higher mentalities (integrity, trust, loyalty) will be missed, and we will demand them from our authorities. Everyone knows what eventually happens to hatchet bosses. They fall on their own hatchets.

Technology has gotten to the point that things become immediately measurable. This can be good or bad, but most seem to think it is a good thing. It is bad to "cheat" the measurements, which we have seen with corporate catastrophes. Nevertheless, we can measure productivity, profitability, and consumer trends more accurately than ever before. If a company is manufacturing something that is losing money and no one wants, they can find out with technology. Management objectives are measured. This can be good in that a manager who is not accomplishing the goals can be replaced. This is bad when the new manager, who may not truly understand the business, has to "cheat" to meet the bottom line. These new technological tools are used both by people with integrity and by burglars. The justice system cannot seem to keep up with the change in technology. At this time the justice system is used by companies to delay the consequences of their unethical but "legal" maneuvers. Americans can take a lot, but when we have had it, we have had it. The patterns of our past indicate that we are not going to be "prostitutes" and "victims" forever.

Technology is now such that a patient can walk into the emergency room at midnight with a broken arm. If there are no doctors available at midnight in the hospital, the x-ray technician can send a copy of the x-ray to a doctor in Australia (where the time is noon). That doctor looks at the x-ray and sends the nurse in the United States the instructions on how to set the arm.

We are incredibly adept at thinking out of the box (part of the reason is because we have so many closet bipolars). In the frontier days, we would cross the country in covered wagons, and if a wheel fell off, we would fix it somehow ("Just do it!"). That is our mentality. When our kids (or adults) whine and cry and say, "I can't . . ." they end up getting kicked in the butt, metaphorically speaking. It is part of our puritanical heritage to work hard. No matter what country our ancestors came from, we ended up here with the values of hard work. People in Europe and the Asian countries follow procedure or cultural values. If a wheel falls off their covered wagon they have a meeting or hire a consultant (usually an American). The Nissan corporation was near failure, and then guess what happened? It was bought by an American company. And then guess what happened? It started making a profit. In the 1960s we were worried about the Germans taking over the world economy (e.g., VW Beetles). Then we worried it was going to be the Arabs in the '70s (oil). Then the Japanese in the '80s (good-quality cars). Then it was the Asian countries (Singapore, Korea, etc.) in the '90s. Now our white-collar jobs are being shifted overseas (India, Philippines, etc.), and our blue-collar jobs are being sent to China, Mexico, and so on. This work that we ship has become "commodity" work. It is standardized with procedure. Many of us with our innovative mentalities and ability to think out of the box don't even like the mundane day-to-day predictable work. We like challenge. We like new stuff. We like having to be inventive. Along with that, we seem to have this cultural fear that drives us to be on top, drives us to make things happen, drives us to go where no one has gone before. The positive thinkers say we are going to be all right—in fact, better than before.

One executive I interviewed thought that human relations has gotten better in large companies. Being nasty can get bosses fired. Lawyers have filed class-action lawsuits that caused companies to come up with training and guidelines from out of their human resources departments. There are no payoffs in being nasty to employees in these companies.

In the workforce, supply and demand can work *for* or *against* an individual. For people who are a "volunteer workforce" (i.e., people who can get a job somewhere else), management has to treat them well. Fostering relationships that work adds to the benefits of management, and creating a culture where people like what they do ensures keeping good people.

Advice from Executives Given This Environment

- If you think your boss is not a good boss, sit down with her or him for a candid talk and present no more than five items for a concrete discussion. Make sure these five things are measurable. If it doesn't happen, transfer or find another job.

- It is hard to be ethical in an unethical world. Maintain your personal integrity, but be as "shrewd as the serpent," as it says in the Bible. Don't assume fairness, nor unfairness. Let trust be earned, not assumed.
- Make sure you negotiate for what you need up front. This is the environment of "promises promises." Get things in writing.
- Do not have any expectations, and you will not have as many disappointments.
- Manage your manager. She or he is also a human being, with similar needs.
- Deception is everywhere. Figure it into your calculations. Your cell phone is going to cost more than they say. There are going to be small charges in your bills that aren't going to be worth your time to correct. The company that hires you is not going to be the "person" you thought. Your boss is not likely to be as presented, and he or she will be limited in power.
- If your boss is a bully, nurture your boss—not out of fear but out of compassion. What bosses do to you is what was done to them. At the same time, do not let the boss degrade you or the boss will lose respect for you. It's simple, but difficult.
- Do not take things personally. It's not about you. Even when it seems like it's about you, it isn't.

- Develop your own charisma. In this environment, you will need it.
- Acknowledge and understand what your boss says first, before you agree or disagree. Make sure the boss knows you understand.
- Treat the boss with respect even when you are going against the boss or your opinion of the boss is low.
- If a better job comes along, take it. In many job environments today, your loyalty and dedication will be unappreciated and may be misperceived as weakness (fear, insecurity, stupidity).
- Put your family first. Your boss is not going to come visit you in the retirement home.
- Network. Connect with other people who may be able to help you. If you are not good at that, learn to be good at that.
- If your skills are becoming obsolete or it looks as if your job may be shipped out of the country, learn a viable skill. You can take an aptitude test at your local community college to see what job would be compatible to your liking and your abilities.
- Even if you do have a good relationship with your boss, don't expect to have this boss forever.
- *Anticipate* your fate before it becomes fateful.
- Communication is still the number one key to success. Communicate. If you can't, learn how (through Dale Carnegie courses, assertiveness training books, etc.).

Advice from the Author

You may find some of the traits in this book in any boss. We are all human and we don't always do the right thing. The biggest key is *do not take it personally*. If you are abused by a nasty boss, that doesn't mean that you should just dust yourself off and continue working. You may need to get out of there, but thinking it is personal just makes it that much worse. The tactics of nasty bosses can be strong. They can make you tend to introvert and become self-conscious. They bring up issues that cause you to have self-doubt. They gossip about you behind your back. They invalidate you and make you look like an ass in front of everyone.

What do we *do* about some of these nasty bosses? There's nothing we can do about Chucky and the Violator, except leave. Others we can work with. Research shows that one of the most significant causes of hostility is a lack of nurturing. Isn't that interesting? So what does the hostile boss need? Nurturing. What is the very thing that you don't feel like giving that boss? Nurturing. But what will work? Nurturing. You did want to know the truth, right? Well, I apologize about the truth, but that doesn't change it. That egotistical, arrogant, entitled boss who always has to be "right" and "win" responds the best to nurturing.

You don't need to take it personally. They are probably doing the same thing to everyone, and that's not personal. Or, you may look like someone who bullied them in the past, and that's not personal.

Pay attention! It's not about you; it's about *them*. Anyone who would use any of these evil mechanisms either has a problem or is simply uncaring about others. Never let anyone introvert you, make you self-conscious, or dominate you. You don't have to. Keep your eye on the source (which is *not* you) and look out there and see them. This person may be going to a lot of effort to dominate you or introvert you. Congratulate them on their efforts in front of everyone. Tell them, "Hey. You are really good. You almost caused me to doubt myself." Or "Wow. You are really powerful. I almost let you dominate me." The secret is not the comeback. The secret is in the PFL. Go to the PFL and stay there when you are being attacked. Look at the big picture. Look at the mammal growling and spitting and jumping up and down (try not to laugh). Trust your gut. Don't let the cognitive mentality introvert. Don't let your mammal attack or run away. Open your third eye (PFL). Things look different from up there. The fact that you can see the bigger picture is usually enough to scare them away. "Hey. What would make you say that to me in front of all these people? What is your purpose in doing that?"

"Gee, I feel like I have just been raped and you guys didn't even touch me. Wow! I am impressed."

"Hey. Your eyes are all bloodshot and your face is all red and you are screaming at me. I am starting to get scared."

"Here. Let me finish your sentence. I am a . . . low-down, good-for-nothing, irresponsible, immature, and worthless human being. Did I get that right?"

I would like to think I invented these comebacks, but I learned them from my son when he was fourteen. He had a good PFL capability at a very early age. I remember that he always used every towel in the bathroom when he took a shower and left them all on the floor. Finally, one day, I had had it. I came in the bathroom and saw all the towels on the floor for the fiftieth time, and I ran down to his room all red in the face and angry. He was calmly sitting at his desk. I yelled at him (but I didn't say what I really wanted to say). Trying to be an objective parent, I said, "Why is it that you have to use every towel in the bathroom and leave them on the floor? Wwwwhhhhyyyyyyy!!!!???" He looked at me (he didn't shy away) and said, "Because I'm an irresponsible little SOB?" He said just what I was thinking but would never say. My anger turned into laughter because he acknowledged me.

You are not always going to get laughter when you expose someone like that, but they won't be inclined to use that trick on you again. And most will leave you alone after you make them psychologically naked.

There are plenty of other approaches that we can discuss. One best one is to develop your very own charisma. Why would you want to do that? Well, it will probably make you feel more like your real self. It will probably greatly enhance your relationships. Other than that, it will probably get you promoted quicker, and then *you* can be the boss!

Keep in mind the bosses who have problems and be kind to them. They don't need you to victimize them. Someone already did, or they wouldn't be doing it to you.

So again,

1. Don't take it personally. It isn't.
2. Maintain your situational awareness. (Do not introvert, become self-conscious, or fall into self-doubt.) Notice the big picture in case you need to feed it back to them. (Don't try to make them eat it, just feed it back.)

Practice

Practice? That's right! Just knowing how you should react to nasty bosses is not enough. You need to practice. You need to practice not introverting. You need to practice not being self-conscious and not having self-doubt. You need to practice nurturing appropriately. Go find someone like your boss and get to know her or him. Go find a bully who needs nurturing and nurture that bully.

When I was writing *Nasty People*, I looked for the best invalidators I could find and tried to hang out with them. I even learned from the ones who didn't want to hang out with me because they invalidated the heck out of me to get rid of me. I noted their techniques, and some of them were real masters at it. I had one invalidator that I had regular access to. He was an in-law (since passed). He was the samurai of the invalidators. I could go to his house prepared, knowing that he was going to try to introvert me and make me feel like a lowlife. He could do it in less than thirty seconds no matter how prepared I was. He was the best. There were no comebacks for some of the things he said to me. Thanks to him, I discovered the ability to just let him do his thing and admire him for it. I told him, "That was really good." When he saw that I knew what he was doing, he got all flustered and left the table. Ah, I realized. The solution is to become bigger than the situation I am in. I didn't realize I was using my PFL at the time, but that's what it was. I was also able to develop a sense of humor. If you are being invalidated by the samurai invalidator, you may as well have a sense of humor about it. I decided to stop being so serious about those nasty, rotten invalidators and practice "humorobics." I ventured out of the intensity of my serious, goal-directed, cognitive quest, and I was finished with being a terminal professional (i.e., dead serious). I couldn't get upset anymore about someone making a fool out of me. Heck, look at me throwing myself on the railroad tracks of an oncoming invalidator. I was a fool, anyway. You know what happens when you throw yourself on the railroad tracks of an oncoming invalidator? Right. The invalidator runs over you. But the train is on a track, and I don't have to be. The invalidator has to ride on the track of the ulterior motive. All I have to do is see the track. People don't like to have their ulterior motives revealed. That's why my in-law left the table.

Again, I have to remind you that some people do not know what their ulterior motives are. They are just repeating what was done to them. They need some empathy and nurturing. They have already been run over by someone else's train.

So practice nurturing and find a nasty person to spend some time with. When you get knocked out of your PFL, get back up there again until you get the hang of it. Practice *not* taking things personally. Look for reasons why it wasn't personal. You don't have to let the situation run over you.

Get busy. Get busy connecting with people, acknowledging people, and finding things to admire about people. Make this your strategy. You will be too busy to introvert, become self-conscious, and have self-doubt. And, who knows, you could be a good boss someday.

Take Action

Above all, keep the bigger picture in sight. From the captain's chair, you can see what lies ahead. Don't get caught up in the small details and introversion of the cognitive mentality. Don't get caught up in the personalization of the mammal feelings. But *do* notice them. Stay alert. Look over the horizon.

From my twenty-five years as a therapist, and having retired from management after twenty-six years, I have compiled the following bottom-line sequence that seems to be helpful to people:

1. **Find or define your purpose in life.** People who have a purpose have more confidence because they know their intent and direction. One executive said, "If you don't know what choice to make, then it is probably so close a decision that it

doesn't matter what decision you make. Just make it and stick with it."

2. **Make sure you prioritize your life so that you can tell the more important things from the less important things.** Do this regularly. Sometimes the list will change. This will help you keep the bigger picture in perspective.

3. **Don't lose sight of your purpose and important things.** Remind yourself every day what your life is about. Don't get sidetracked.

4. **Become bigger than your problems.** If you "can't" or you don't know how, hang out with someone who *can* and *does*. It rubs off. Don't try to do it *all* yourself. No man or woman is an island. Swallow your pride, show a little humility, and ask for help. It's good for the soul.

5. **Find a mentor and an advisory board.** Find someone who has your best interest in mind and can be objective (sponsor, therapist, best friend, etc.). Find a good set of friends (advisory board) with varied backgrounds.

6. **Be a mentor. Be an adviser.** It will give you practice mentoring and advising *yourself*.

Leaving You in the Lobe

Now pay attention. This is the end of the book and the most important part. Are you in your prefrontal lobe? Ready to see a big picture? OK, here we go.

First, find a bathroom and go in. Make sure it has a mirror.

Ready? Look in the mirror. You see that person there?

That's the boss. And I bet you thought it was someone else, huh?

All the decisions you have made in your life have finally led you to this moment in this bathroom. This is how your life turned out.

Follow me slowly now. There is more.

Why did you pick up this book, *Nasty Bosses*? Because you feel a little powerless with regard to someone? C'mon, admit it. You do feel a little powerless or maybe a lot powerless. And maybe you wanted some magic trick to handle a situation so you could regain your sense of power.

What if I could show you a way to regain that power without any tricks or clever comebacks or a menu of exercises? Would you want that? If so, keep reading.

If I could show you that, it would have to be an irrefutable truth that you would have to be prepared to *see*. You wouldn't be able to "think" it in; you would have to really *see* it as an awareness of something that already exists in truth. You would have to be in a state of mind to see the big picture of it—the whole of it.

There might not be a word for it, because it might be beyond words, but we would have to use words because that's all that's available at this moment.

Here's the first part. Just hold this in the palm of your hand for now. I am not asking you to believe it, just *see* it.

Some say, "With great power comes great responsibility."

The reverse may be even more true.

"With great responsibility comes great power."

Responsibility is a choice. If my neighbors' house gets struck by lightning it is not my fault and I am not to blame, but I can take total responsibility for it and fix it if I so choose.

People say that the secrets to success are communication and a willingness to take responsibility.

With me so far?

Here's the paradox. (A paradox is something that can be true but seems conflicting.)

The paradox is: you are totally responsible for everything that happens to you, whether you believe it or not, whether you like it or not, whether it's fair or not, and whether you are aware of it or not. If I shoot you, yes it's my fault, but you are going to end up being the one who is responsible. Whose body did the bullet go through? Yours. Who may die? You. You end up being responsible, whether you like it or not, whether it's fair or not, whether you are aware of it or not, and whether you believe it or not. It's almost a cosmic joke. We don't take responsibility for a lot of things, yet we are responsible for them anyway—whether we believe it or not, like it or not, and so on.

Here's the kicker. If you *know* you are responsible anyway, you will choose to take responsibility. You will bandage the bullet wound. Then you may not bleed to death. If you take no responsibility, you may just walk off saying, "This is not my fault. I didn't do this. I am not going to deal with it." Then you will bleed to death.

When I was young and my prefrontal lobe hadn't been developed yet, a friend of mine showed up in the front of my house, drunk. He asked me if I wanted to go for a ride in his new hot car. The mammal part of me (sensing danger) said, "No." Then he appealed to my logic and said, "C'mon, Carter. I have good insurance and seat belts. I will take total responsibility for anything that happens to you." Like a dummy, I said, "OK!" But what if I were a paraplegic from an accident? Could he take responsibility for that? It wouldn't matter how much insurance money I got.

So that's the basic truth of it then. You are responsible for everything that happens, and to regain your power, you need to take responsibility for the things you are already responsible for anyway.

An older woman was doing one of my seminars, and she said that she really needed to know the universal truth that I just gave to you (whether you received it or not). She said it would have helped her if she had realized it earlier, but she appreciated it greatly. Then she called me a bastard with a smile on her face. It sucks to realize you are totally responsible, but it does give you the power back.

I can vouch for that. I have a personal example.

At one point in my life, it seemed I was surrounded by invalidators. People would put me down constantly—my boss, my professor, my significant other. I was sinking lower and lower and "they" were doing it to me. I refused to be like "them" and do it back. My self-esteem was shot. The more I spiraled downward, the more people joined the bandwagon. Even my peers at work were joining my evil boss in the carping criticisms and cruel jokes at my expense. I was stressed out. These dirty rotten people kept putting me down and making me miserable, and then some "jerk" tried to tell me *I* was responsible for it. Hah!

But as insane as it sounded to my cognitive mentality, my "big picture" self saw some truth in it. First, I studied the invalidators closely and watched how they did it. I even provoked the invalidation so I could study it. Then I wrote down and documented the techniques. I was going to write a book called *The Invalidator* and expose all those dirty creeps. I gave this book to a friend to read. He was the nicest guy in the world. He came back the next day with tears in his eyes and said, "I do this to my mother. How can I stop?" I was floored. I realized I had written only half a book. At first I was going to take responsibility by beating up these people in my book. Then I went to the next level of responsibility by trying to help those "invalidators" who wanted to stop. Finally, one day, I decided I was going to take responsibility for invalidation in the world. By that time I was realizing some things because I was *willing* to be responsible. I started realizing that wearing green knit shirts, sporting a beard, and wearing a plaid tie in corporate America in the '70s may have had something to do with the ribbing I got. I realized that coming home late without calling my wife may have had something to do with her desire to verbally beat me up. My professor did not stop invalidating me, but when I looked at the big picture and saw that she did it to everyone, it didn't seem so personal. She just had a character flaw. Once I took responsibility for it, the invalidation stopped. I started asking questions I had never asked before like, "What might *I* be doing to cause this?" My book *Nasty People* has sold more than a million copies around the world. Have I stopped invalidation in the world yet? Not yet. I have gotten to only a million people, so far.

So after all this, let me ask you some questions that possibly haven't been asked.

Are you willing to take responsibility for your nasty boss?

If your answer is no, read the book again.

What are you doing to cause your boss to be nasty?

Maybe your existence alone is causing the boss to be nasty. If so, you probably shouldn't do anything to change yourself. Otherwise, there may be some things you can choose to take responsibility for that you haven't assumed responsibility for . . . yet. If you don't ask how you are responsible, you don't do your part.

Now that you are responsible for your nasty boss, you may want to write me a nasty letter or a nice letter. You can reach me at my website:

jaycarter.net

or write to me at:

P.O. Box 6048
Wyomissing, PA 19610

I also do speaking engagements on these topics:

Executive Functions for Executives (Prefrontal Lobe)
Gender Issues in the Workplace
Anger Management
Mental Health Issues in the Workplace

Bibliography

Alberti, Robert. *Your Perfect Right*. San Luis Obispo, CA: Impact, 1981.

American Psychiatric Association. *Diagnostic and Statistical Manual of Mental Disorders DSM-IV* (4th ed). Washington, DC: Author, 2000.

American Psychological Association. *Warning Signs*. Washington, DC: Author, 2000.

Beattie, Melody. *Codependent No More: How to Stop Controlling Others and Start Caring for Yourself* (2nd edition). Center City, MN: Hazelden, 1997.

Berry, Carmen Renee. *When Helping You Is Hurting Me*. San Francisco: Harper & Row, 1988.

Bly, Robert. *Iron John*. New York: Addison-Wesley, 1990.

Carlson, Richard. *Don't Sweat the Small Stuff*. New York: Hyperion, 1997.

Carter, Jay. *Bipolar: An Unorthodox Approach*. Wyomissing, PA: Unicorn Press, 2001.

Carter, Jay. *Nasty People* (revised edition). Chicago: Contemporary Books, 2003.

Dempsey, Mary H., and Tihista, Renee. *Dear Job Stressed*. Palo Alto, CA: Davies-Black Publishing, 1996.

Ellis, Albert, and Harper, Robert A. *A New Guide to Rational Living*. Princeton, NJ: Prentice Hall, 1975.

Ellis, Albert, and Tafrate, Raymond. *How to Control Your Anger Before It Controls You*. New York: Citadel Press, 1997.

Gibran, Kahlil. *The Treasured Writings of Kahlil Gibran*. Edison, NJ: Castle Books, 1995.

Gray, John. *Men Are from Mars, Women Are from Venus*. New York: HarperCollins, 1992.

Hallowell, Edward M., and Ratey, John J. *Driven to Distraction*. New York: Touchstone, 1994.

Hare, Robert. *Without Conscience*. New York: Guildford Press, 1993.

Johnson, Spencer. *One Minute Manager*. New York: Berkeley Books, 1983.

Johnson, Spencer. *Who Moved My Cheese?* New York: Putnam & Sons, 1998.

Kaufman, Phyllis C., and Corrigan, Arnold. *Managing People, at Work, at Home*. Stanford, CT: Longmeadow Press, 1988.

Kidd, Sue Monk. *The Secret Life of Bees.* New York: Penguin Books, 2002.

Kiersey, David. *Please Understand Me II.* Del Mar, CA: Prometheus, 1998.

Lewis, C. S. *The Screwtape Letters.* New York: MacMillan, 1961.

McKay, Matthew, and Rogers, Peter. *The Anger Control Workbook.* Oakland, CA: New Harbinger Publications, 2000.

Metcalf, Ceu. "Humor." Presentation at the Inn at Reading, PA: June 2, 1994.

Miller, Alice. *Prisoners of Childhood.* New York: Basic Books, 1981.

"Miss Manners Regrets." *BusinessWeek,* January 12, 2004. businessweek.com:/print/magazine/content/04_02/b38 65742.htm?mz.

Mondimore, Francis Mark. *Bipolar Disorder: A Guide for Patients and Families.* Baltimore: Johns Hopkins Press, 1999.

Payne, Robert. *The Life and Death of Adolf Hitler.* New York: Praeger Publishers, 1973.

Peck, M. Scott. *People of the Lie.* New York: Touchstone, 1983.

Persig, Robert. *Zen and the Art of Motorcycle Maintenance*. New York: Bantam, 1981.

Rathus, Spencer A. *Essentials of Psychology*. Fort Worth, TX: Harcourt Brace, 1997.

Tannen, Deborah. *You Just Don't Understand*. New York: Ballantine, 1990.

Toffler, Alvin. *Future Shock*. New York: Bantam Books, 1970.

Watts, Alan. *Ego*. Berkeley, CA: Celestial Arts Publishing, 1975.

Watts, Alan. *Time*. Berkeley, CA: Celestial Arts Publishing, 1975.

Wilde, Jerry. *The Anger Management Book*. Richmond, IN: LGR Publishing, 1997.

Williams, Redfield, and Jamison, Kay Redfield. *Anger Kills*. New York: Harper Torch, 1998.